SPEECHPOWER

SPEECHPOWER

Communicating with clarity, confidence
and conviction

Gabriel J. Hunt
BA, HDipEd, ATCL, MSc (Mgmt)

Signum Books
Dublin

First published 1984
by Signum Books
60 Sweetmount Park, Dublin 14, Ireland

Designed by Jarlath Hayes.

British Library Cataloguing in Publication Data

Hunt, Gabriel J.
    Speechpower : communicating with clarity,
    confidence and conviction.
    1. Public speaking
    I. Title
    808.5'1   PN4121

ISBN 0 9509778 0 2 H/B.
ISBN 0 9509778 1 0 Pbk.

Photoset in Baskerville and
printed by Mount Salus Press, Dublin

Contents

Preface and Acknowledgements

This book deals with most aspects of spoken communication. In it I have included what I feel the 'all round' speaker should know about this subject so that he or she will be able to speak effectively on any given occasion — thereby furthering personal development.

I pay particular attention to 'the mind behind the voice', for I believe the inner should powerfully guide the outer. I have, therefore, included some chapters on this theme.

Most of the techniques throughout the book can be studied and applied by practically everyone, because life is communication and communication skills apply universally. To do a common thing uncommonly well brings success — so also with communication.

I wish to express my heartfelt thanks to Miss Ursula Belotti, Dr Liam Gorman, Dr Margaret Mac Curtain, Dr Mícheál Mac Gréil S.J. and Mr Tom Ronayne for their reading of the original manuscript and for their valuable suggestions, many of which have been incorporated into this book.

I owe a special word of thanks to my good friend Dr Oliver Powell for his unfailing help, support and encouragement whilst the book was being written. For his kind assistance in guiding the book through its final stages, I am deeply grateful.

To my wife Teresa, I owe a very special debt of gratitude — this book would not have been possible without her constant encouragement, inspiration, and constructive criticisms, offered from the very beginning. To her also, my thanks for the arduous task of typing and re-typing the various drafts of the manuscript.

Finally, to my late parents, who never failed to encourage me in my professional career, my sincere thanks.

August 1984   Gabriel J. Hunt
                                        60 Sweetmount Park
                                              Dublin 14

To Teresa, Trevor and Alfred

Introduction

To every thing there is a season, and a
time to every purpose under the heaven . . .
A time to keep silence and a time to speak . . .
— ECCLESIASTES 3:1-8

On 28 August 1963, a great speaker focused the minds of a
nation when he addressed a massive civil rights demonstration in
Washington, D.C. In his speech on that day, Dr Martin Luther
King Jnr repeated the phrase 'I have a dream' with such an
intensity of conviction and feeling that millions were moved by
his eloquence.

Most great speakers have a dream. This dream is born of a
great conviction and it is communicated in a way that inspires
people to do great things. Daniel O'Connell (1775-1847), the
Irish 'Liberator', who opposed violence as a means of achieving
his political objectives, was a silver-tongued 'dreamer' who
moved the Irish Nation towards Catholic Emancipation (1829).
He addressed open-air meetings throughout Ireland and it is
said that tens of thousands could hear his powerful voice as he
delivered his speeches — there were no microphones in those
days. A quarter of a million people came to hear him speak at
Tara, the home of the ancient kings of Ireland. Indeed,
O'Connell himself was often referred to at the time as the
'Uncrowned King of Ireland'.

Another 'dreamer' was John Fitzgerald Kennedy. His
message was that of 'hope' and he was a leader with whom the
young at that time could relate. It is said that JFK's greatest
contribution to history was the 'leadership of hope'. People all
over the world looked up to Kennedy because he too was looking
up . . . he had a dream. And he spoke about that dream.

The Cradle of Oratory

Great oratory formally began in Athens four hundred years
before Christ. One of the ancient Greeks, Demosthenes, reputed
to have been one of the greatest orators of all time, is particularly

famous for his great speech 'On The Crown' (330 B.C.). In this masterful speech, Demosthenes brilliantly defended his public life against charges made by his political rival Aeschines. These charges maintained that Demosthenes had no right to the golden crown granted to him for his services to Athens. How Demosthenes became a great speaker is related elsewhere in this book.

The Greeks believed in the development of the 'Whole Person' and the supreme manifestation of this ideal was in the perfect orator. They used the power of speech and thought so effectively that Athens became the cultural centre of the western world. The great orators were educated in the arts, politics and philosophy. These studies served them well when they spoke in any of the three areas of oratory prevalent at the time — Legal Oratory, Political Oratory and Ceremonial Oratory. The two main books on oratory were Plato's *Phaedrus* (c.380 B.C.) and Aristotle's *Rhetoric* (c.330 B.C.).

The Greeks influenced the Romans and so oratory also blossomed in Rome. The greatest Roman orator was Cicero (106-43 B.C.), who, along with his fellow orators, spoke in the Roman Forum where the citizens debated and settled the problems of the day. The Romans also wrote books on the education of the orator, for example, Cicero's *De Oratore* (55 B.C.) and Quintilian's *Institutio Oratoria* (A.D. 95).

Greek and Roman oratory then influenced the early Christian Church. The principles of oratory as enunciated by Aristotle and Cicero were used by Church leaders such as St Augustine (354-430) to argue against various rival doctrines. The principles also flourished throughout the Middle Ages when Pope Urban II in 1095 and St Bernard of Clairvaux in 1144 used their oratorical abilities to urge on those taking part in the crusades.

Coming down the centuries we had great speakers like Joan of Arc, Martin Luther, John Wesley, Robert Emmet, Abraham Lincoln, Patrick H. Pearse, Mahatma Gandhi, Franklin D. Roosevelt, Sir Winston Churchill, Gamal Abd'el Nasser, to name just a few. Each of these had a dream, and each had the ability to communicate their dream with clarity, confidence, and conviction.

Models of Greatness

Great speakers whom we admire can be models to hold before our mind's eye. And why not? For everyone can aspire to become a really good speaker — and some can aspire to join the ranks of the 'greats', especially if they have the essential ingredient of a great speaker, that is, a dream or vision founded on some great conviction. Many people, however, fear speaking in front of an audience — especially the beginners because to them it is an unknown situation. What is required is courage — the courage to begin. George Bernard Shaw is a classic example. As a young man, he was very shy. He decided, however, to conquer his shyness by availing of every opportunity that came his way of standing up and delivering a talk. He forced himself to speak at the Fabian Society in London. By having the courage to begin, and by forcing himself to address audiences, he overcame his extreme shyness and was later to speak in some of the largest halls in London. He was also much in demand as an after-dinner speaker.

The Power of Speech

Many people who have the courage to take that initial step as Shaw did, discover that in projecting their voice to an audience, they are freed from speaking inhibitions. In learning to accept the sound of their own voice they begin to feel a sense of self-confidence, power, and leadership in sharing their thoughts and feelings with an audience. Having an audience to convince also leads the conscientious speaker into preparing a definite message. This preparation helps the speaker to clarify his or her mind on the essential points of a topic and to see the various relationships inherent in them. Economy in the use of words is also learned because the speaker develops the habit of matching a message against a given time. The ideas that are expressed out loud in the form of a talk also become more meaningful for the speaker. When we verbalise self-selected ideas, they become more a part of our being. We internalise or take ownership of these ideas.

Finally, holding the attention of an audience develops in the speaker a healthy appreciation of his or her own quality and worth as a person. This self-confidence can then become the doorway to many other achievements in his or her personal, business, social, political, and community life.

The Acorn of Oratory

The above facts have a profound implication for the classroom. Perhaps they are best summed up in the maxim — 'You don't really understand something until you can explain it to someone else'. This maxim tends to be forgotten by those educators who concentrate exclusively on imparting facts, rather than giving students an opportunity to give verbal expression to those facts through formal speaking and debating. More verbal expression in the classroom through training students how to give effective talks on the various subjects they are studying would help them to clarify their thoughts and convictions on the knowledge they are acquiring.

Abraham Lincoln's Secret

Abraham Lincoln (1809-1865) was a great speaker who understood the value of the above maxim. His world famous 'Gettysburg Oration' is reproduced in the chapter entitled 'A Masterpiece of Simplicity and Brevity'. Lincoln himself had very little formal education. He was largely self-taught and his main reading was the Bible, Shakespeare, and Euclid. He was once asked what was the secret of his effective speaking — how did he acquire his unique, clear, and powerful way of 'putting things'. Lincoln replied . . .

Among my earliest recollections, I remember how, when a mere child, I used to get irritated when anybody talked to me in a way I could not understand. I can remember going to my little bedroom, after hearing the neighbours talk of an evening with my father, and spending no small part of the night walking up and down, and trying to make out what was the exact meaning of some of their, to me, dark sayings. I could not sleep, though I often tried to, when I got on such a hunt after an idea, until I had caught it; and when I thought I had got it, I was not satisfied until I had repeated it over and over, until I had put it in language plain enough, as I thought, for any boy I knew to comprehend. This was a kind of passion with me, and it has stuck by me.

The Two Principles of Leadership

This principle of verbalising ideas and convictions is very important in any leadership training programme (business, community, youth, political). Effective leadership training is based on two principles. The first of these is to teach a person special knowledge, make the person a specialist in something. The second principle is to teach that person how to communicate that special knowledge. Unfortunately, however, the second principle is sometimes forgotten and so poor leadership is the result. Many specialists are not trained speakers. An effective leadership training programme will teach participants how to become fluent in communicating the essentials of a message with clarity, confidence, and conviction. For fluency is the art that conceals art, and it is the stage — in whatever walk of life — that distinguishes the really competent from the mediocre communicator.

Community Action

Effective speaking also has a vital role to play in community action, for effective speaking and action are intertwined. There is a need for more and more people to become actively involved in their local community organisations, in local politics, in church affairs. The more people who speak up effectively, the healthier it is for democracy. A healthy democracy is a nation of people talking to people and exercising as much local control as possible over the vital decisions that affect their lives. The 'silent majority' becomes an articulate majority with the verbal power to get things done in their community. Democracy demands that each person speaks up with the courage of his or her convictions when the occasion demands.

The Time to Speak — Is Now

The ancient Greeks, as mentioned earlier, believed in the development of the 'Whole Person'. They envisaged oratory as playing a major role in all of this development. Their ideal of developing great thinkers and speakers is still valid, and indeed even vital, in our own day when we need to express our beliefs and convictions about the various issues which confront us daily in this world of rapid change. The alternative to not thinking for ourselves and to not expressing our thoughts is that others will do our thinking for us. An art of oratory which is built upon a personal quest for truth will help us to keep alive the ideal of those ancient Greeks.

So the time to speak is now. Everyone, no matter how experienced or inexperienced in the art of oratory, can aim to become a more effective communicator in whatever his or her walk of life. So why not grasp the speaking opportunities as they present themselves? For just as the little acorn can become the great oak tree, so also can great speakers arise from small beginnings in the art of oratory.

Part One

THE MIND BEHIND THE VOICE

I think, therefore I am.
— RENÉ DESCARTES

1 Know thyself – speaking with conviction

If the trumpet gives an uncertain sound,
who shall prepare himself to the battle.
— 1 CORINTHIANS 14:8

Imagine you are walking down a busy street and a TV interviewer sticks a microphone in front of you and asks you this question: 'Tell me, Sir/Madam, what are your basic convictions?' Would they come trippingly on your tongue? A great number of people have never formally articulated their personal beliefs or principles. They have never really looked deeply within themselves to discover what they believe about the vital issues that affect their lives. Because of this, their speaking can lack that quality of depth, force and courage which is the offspring of conviction — the foundation stone of powerful speaking.

The aim of this chapter, therefore, is to help you discover, formulate, and deepen your personal convictions. The rest of the book is designed mainly to help you communicate those convictions in the most interesting, meaningful, and effective way. Let us now consider the theme of conviction in some detail.

Self-Discovery and Convictions

A man who bows down to nothing
can never bear the burden of himself.
— DOSTOIEVSKI

Psychologists tell us that as human beings our potential for growth is enormous. Indeed it is far greater than we can possibly imagine and, unfortunately, we only use a very small percentage of that potential. My own belief is that formulating and expressing our own personally held convictions plays a major part in all of this development. We personally grow and discover ourselves as we look inwards to formulate our convictions and as we look outwards to express them. Giants of men and women

17

down through the ages are recognised as having been people of great conviction.

So, what is conviction? To have a conviction and to speak with conviction means that you are convinced about something, that you have a strong belief about something, that you are sure about something and that you courageously express those beliefs. However, before I help you to gain a deeper insight into your own convictions, and perhaps to formulate some new ones, let us look at some of the major advantages of having self-formulated convictions. First of all, let us consider their relation to life's meaning and the above quote from Dostoievski.

Many people, especially those with a philosophical inclination, ask the question: What is life all about? What is the. meaning of existence? Indeed great minds have often gone mad wondering why we are here on this planet. One writer, George Santayana (1863-1952), in trying to answer the question has said: 'Man is not made to understand life, but to live it.' This may or may not be so. Indeed some readers may find his answer too simplistic. Perhaps it is too broad a question to ask in the first place. But there is one thing of which I feel we can be certain, namely, that if we formulate our basic convictions, verbalise them, and live our lives by them as well as we can, our lives will have more meaning, a better sense of direction, and a richer feeling of fulfilment.

When we psychologically commit ourselves to our personal convictions, we leave less time for the burden of apathy and bored living. Indeed we become truly free, because ultimately freedom must surely be obedience to self-formulated rules, personal commandments or guidelines we have established for leading our own life.

Convictions in an Age of Uncertainty

To have self-formulated convictions is vital in today's complicated world of rapid change where some of the old 'certitudes' that formerly gave meaning to people's lives are being questioned. The older person may say: 'I don't know what to believe any more.' As someone amusingly put it: 'The trouble with our times is that the future is not what it used to be.' Young people, on the other hand, may be tempted to tear down, indiscriminately, the old fabric of society and experiment dangerously with some of the dark alleyways of life. And all of this without a clear conviction and understanding of what, ultimately, he or she really wants in life. Young people, therefore, should be encouraged to formulate and express their personal convictions about today's vital issues. We shall have a look at some of these issues further on in this chapter.

I like to think of convictions as mental anchors. Just as a ship needs an anchor to keep it steady, secure and free from drifting on to the rocks, so also do we need mental anchors to keep us steady in this world of rapid change. The mental anchor of our convictions gives our lives an inner strength. In *Man and Superman* George Bernard Shaw sums up this internal feeling of strength and well-being which comes from having convictions: 'This is the true joy in life, the being used for a purpose recognised by yourself as a mighty one.' The alternative is purposeless drift — a bouncing from one unplanned event to the next as we are swept along by the straw of circumstances and uncertainty.

This age of uncertainty in which we live constantly demands rapid and effective decision-making as we face new crises, new challenges, new opportunities. Our convictions can play a major role in effective decision-making, as we shall now see. The lack of them can lead ultimately to procrastination.

Convictions and Decision-Making

Let me ask you a few questions. As you examine these you may recognise some of your own tendencies when it comes to decision-making. Do you find making decisions a difficult task? Do you get bogged down in detail? Do you tend to put off making decisions hoping they will go away? This may succeed for a time but chickens have a habit of coming home to roost. Do you avoid decisions by overqualifying things out of existence? This can be a habit of the over-academically detached person who tends to seek a certain comfortable refuge in ambiguity. As Herbert Spencer put it: 'When a man's knowledge is not in order, the more of it he has, the greater will be his confusion.'

Do you constantly use certain phrases which can reinforce a tendency to procrastinate, for example: 'It all depends'; 'There

is much to be said on both sides'; 'I need to think this through.'
Whilst the use of such phrases is quite valid at times, their *overuse*,
however, might become a camouflage for those decisions you
really need to make, and you might also appear to others as not
knowing your own mind.

Are you afraid of making a decision because it involves
conflict? Recognise that all decisions involve some conflict. Are
you afraid of making a bad decision? However, is there ever such
a thing as a perfect decision?

These are some of the symptoms of procrastination. But, why
do we procrastinate and what can we do about it? I have often
pondered on the meaning of Shakespeare's phrase 'To thine own
self be true'. What is the *self* in this quotation? Is there some
constant *self*? Some philosophical writers say there are many
different 'I''s within each of us and this makes us prone to
indecision. One of our 'I''s inwardly says *yes* to something whilst
some other 'I' says *no* at the same time. The result can be inner
and outer confusion. Formulating our convictions, however, can
help us to integrate these many 'I''s of indecision into a whole or
unified person who knows his or her own mind. Our convictions
can give a sort of permanency or personal identity to our *self*.
We then know where we stand on various vital issues (career,
religion, family, politics, etc.) because we have the reference
point of our convictions as a guide.

Whenever you have an important decision to make, ask
yourself: Would this goal or proposed course of action conflict
with my basic convictions? What do my convictions tell me to do
in this situation? From the point of view of my convictions how
should I judge this matter? How many of the pros and cons come
nearest to my convictions?

Convictions and Energy

I recently watched a TV series of in-depth interviews with
well-known successful people from various spheres of life. The
major thing that struck me about these people was their
tremendous energy and their conviction and dedication to their
chosen careers. There seemed to be a strong link between their
energy level and their degree of conviction. Convictions have
that powerful effect of giving us the mental energy to get things

done. They keep us motivated and mentally alive. In this regard, it is worth bearing in mind that whenever you feel mentally drained and tired, one cause might well be that you no longer are motivated or convinced about what you are doing. Some re-thinking may be in order.

The mental energy of our convictions can see us through all sorts of difficulties and enable us to tackle them with courage. Assessing decisions against the criteria of our convictions, as already recommended, can also enable us to economise on the amount of energy we use in the decision-making process. Procrastination tires, frustrates, and saps away energy.

Finally, it is worth remembering that any group of committed people with their accompanying energies can revitalise any 'tired' organisation, community, political party, or business company.

Formulating Your Convictions

We have seen in the previous paragraphs the many advantages of having convictions. So, hopefully having 'whetted your appetite', now is the opportune time to look into your heart to formulate or examine your convictions and to study how you might give expression to them in everyday life. From my communications and motivational work with individuals and groups, I have come up with a broad list of convictions as examples for you to ponder on. Agree or disagree with these as you think fit. I have grouped the examples under various headings and I pose a number of questions on each topic. Use the questions as a springboard to stimulate your thinking on what you already believe, or might come to believe, about some vital issues facing us today. First of all, let us look at convictions about yourself.

Self

Have you ever asked what are your convictions about yourself as a person? Have you assessed your strengths and weaknesses? Have you a conviction to reach your full potential? To express what you do best? To use your talents to the full? To be really good at something? Do you have a personal conviction to learn all through your life — not only from successes but also from

failures? Consider: 'Bad times have a scientific value. These are occasions a good learner would not miss.' *Ralph Waldo Emerson.*
Do you believe in ambition, in setting goals? If so, what are your ambitions? Does goal-setting destroy 'living in the present' and take away from the spontaneity of life? Consider: 'Although it is a good scriptural injunction to live a day at a time, you will never really manage that unless you have a concept of tomorrow.' *Lord Soper.*
What is your conviction about your appearance and how you present yourself to others? Personal cleanliness is above all a signal that you care about yourself. That you appreciate yourself. You also value and appreciate yourself when you exercise your body, take rest, care about the right kind and amount of food you eat. Finally, are you convinced that you are a worthwhile person? This is the fundamental conviction. It presents us from destroying our lives in any way. Remember that people take you at your own evaluation of yourself. So project outwardly with courage and confidence your inner belief in your own value as a person. Be yourself and express that fact with great conviction.
Let us now consider the subject of convictions insofar as they touch on some of the wider aspects of life. We live more fully when we are aware of what is going on in the wider world around us in all those areas that impinge on our lives. What future do we want to create for ourselves, our families, our community, the world?

Religion/Morality
Do you believe in a God, a Creative Force, an Absolute? Do you believe in a Personal God? An after-life? Free-will? What about fate? Do you believe in prayer? Do you believe in attending church, mosque, synagogue, temple? What about ecumenism? Why are you a believer, an atheist, or an agnostic?
What about the right to life? Do you believe in abortion? And genetic engineering? What about euthanasia? And capital punishment? What is conscience? And an informed conscience? Do you have a conviction about following your conscience in all things? Do you think it is important to do your duty as you conceive it regardless of what people may think, say, or do?

Consider: 'Do not believe anything because the written testimony of some ancient wise man is shown to you. Whatever accords with your own experience and after thorough investigation agrees with your reason — that accept as truth and live accordingly.' *Buddha.*

What are your convictions about human nature? What about the notion of evil? Do you believe that good triumphs over evil? Do you have a conviction about the infliction of mental and physical suffering on people? And also on animals? Does the end justify the means?

Family

Do you believe in marriage? Can you defend it as an institution? Do we have a duty to aged parents? What about the idea of the extended family? How valid is the fourth commandment? Do you believe in divorce, birth control, trial marriages? Should parents be responsible for the vandalism of their children? And for the morality of their young children?

Do you believe in family life? In being open with your parents/spouse/children? When you say, 'I love you', do you really mean it, or is it an embarrassed squawk? Consider: Convictions, like charity, should begin at home. To argue for the larger causes whilst neglecting self and family is a mockery.

Work

As we spend so much of our time at work, it is a useful exercise to examine what convictions we have about this aspect of our life. What are your convictions about the nature of work in general, the work ethic, success, private enterprise, the quality of life versus work, working at home? Have you goals for your career? Do you believe in risk-taking?

What convictions have you about your company? About its products or service? Do you have a conviction that you want to succeed in your company? What are its strengths and weaknesses? Do you have a conviction about the job you hold? Ask yourself: What three main convictions about this job will guide my decision-making? Do you maintain a daily interest in your work? What convictions have you about trades unions? About multinationals? About unemployment? And the various solutions often proposed (work-sharing, early retirement, etc.)? Do you believe in separating work from family life? How do you feel about promotion at the possible risk to health and family life?

Local Community

Do you believe in helping your local community? Have you considered becoming involved in your local residents' association, parish council, local charities, youth club, community centre? How about helping your neighbour? Do you believe in protecting your local environment from pollution, crime, vandalism, litter, drugs? Consider: 'One thing I know, the only ones among you who will be really happy are those who have sought and found how to serve.' *Dr Albert Schweitzer.*

Country

To what extent should we love our country? Do you have any strong feelings about your country? How much do you know about its past, its traditions, its culture? To what extent should these be preserved? Do you believe in supporting home industry? Consider: 'Ask not what your country can do for you, ask what you can do for your country.' *John F. Kennedy.* If you were to act the prophet, what future would you like to see for your country in the next ten years?

World

What would you like to see for the world? Are we doing enough for world hunger, poverty, refugees, disasters? These are 'miles away', should we concentrate instead on local charities? Can we support both? Do you support a relief organisation?

What about nuclear disarmament? Do you believe in the following: the E.E.C., the U.N., N.A.T.O.? What about neutrality? How much do you know about Amnesty International? Why is there racial prejudice? Consider: 'To ignore the danger is to deserve the disaster.' *Anon.* 'Three passions, simple but overwhelmingly strong, have governed my life — the longing for love, the search for knowledge and unbearable pity for the sufferings of mankind.' *Bertrand Russell.*

Politics

How interested are you in politics? Have you any political convictions? Asking this question reminds me of a little anecdote. A young man was considering entering politics but was unsure of his convictions and which party he should join. He mentioned to his father that he would stick on his head a label saying *To let* and that he would join whichever party offered him the most. 'Do that', said his father, 'but don't forget to write on the label the word *Unfurnished.*'

As politics affects us in every detail of our lives, can we afford to be lookers-on, 'unfurnished', so to speak? Consider: 'Don't let it happen, it depends on you.' *George Orwell.*

Do you think politics is a dirty game, or do you agree with the following?: 'Public life is the crown of a career, and to young men it is the worthiest ambition. Politics is still the greatest and most honourable adventure.' *Lord Tweedsmuir.* Should you steer away from politics and its accompanying power because it might tend to corrupt (some) people and possibly you? What should be the essential role of the politician?

What is the difference between a politician and a statesman? How true is this saying?: 'A politician thinks only of the next election; a statesman thinks of the next generation.' Have you ever considered giving expression to your political convictions by joining a political party? Why not list the major political issues of the day as you see them (local, national, international) and practise speaking on them, using your basic convictions as a reference point? Which political party and party political manifesto comes nearest to your convictions?

What are your beliefs about the women's liberation movement? Do you believe in a caring society? How could it be more caring? Do you see any area of oppression that needs rectifying and in which you can play a part? Consider: 'One's individual survival requires that one throw in one's weight on behalf of the emerging, healthy forces of society.' *Harvey Jackins.*

Do you believe in upholding the values of the past and integrating them with the progress of today? Do you believe in evolution in society or in revolution to achieve change? What are your convictions about individual freedom and freedom of speech? How far can it go? Do you believe in the right of law? What is righteous law?

Integrating Your Convictions

Why not bring all of your convictions together and compile your own brief statement of the direction you would like to see society taking? Reflecting on all of the areas of your convictions can help you to formulate your own personal manifesto.

You will grow as a person if you speak up about your faith in the things you consider worthwhile in life. This demands courage.

Having the Courage of Your Convictions

Once you have formulated your convictions, you should give expression or witness to them as the occasion demands. There should be no dissimilarity between them and your way of life. This is amusingly illustrated in the words of an anonymous poem:

> *There was a dachshund once, so long*
> *He hadn't any notion*
> *How long it took to notify*
> *His tail of his emotion;*
> *And so it happened, while his eyes*
> *Were filled with woe and sadness,*
> *His little tail went wagging on*
> *Because of previous gladness.*

Most people will respect you for stating your convictions forcefully, courageously, and as plainly as you can. They may sometimes disagree with your views, but they will admire your courage and integrity when you behave from your own convictions rather than simply tagging along. When your convictions are put to the test, your need to maintain your own self-respect and integrity is more important than any momentary popularity with others. In his inspiring book, *Profiles in Courage,* John F. Kennedy wrote: 'A man does what he must — in spite of personal consequences, in spite of obstacles and dangers and pressures — and that is the basis of all human morality.'

The ultimate example of personal conviction must surely be that displayed by those people, who, even in the face of possible death, draw tremendous courage from their convictions. Another example of conviction is that expressed by people such as Mother Teresa of Calcutta. Such people, whose very presence is often a message in itself, when asked where they will get the money to build a church, a hospital, an orphanage, are often heard to say, 'God will provide.' Attitudes such as these reflect the singlemindedness of conviction. The exiled writer, Solzhenitsyn, speaking of his homeland, Russia, when he was interviewed on a TV programme said: 'I live with this single conviction: I shall return.' Pope John Paul II in expressing a conviction said: 'I am convinced they cheer not myself, but the successor of Peter.'

Our convictions should lead to action. This means that we are not ashamed or afraid to express our convictions as the occasion demands. So, if you feel happy about something, don't be afraid to show it. If you believe in God, don't be afraid to say so. If you're an atheist, don't be afraid to reveal it. If you believe in success and the work ethic, express it. If you love your wife/husband/parents, show it. If you believe in a caring society, prove it. If you believe in your products or service, go all out to sell them. Expressing our convictions in everyday life provides a great opportunity to test our capacity for courage. We also gain deeper insights into our convictions the more we verbalise them. Finally, remember: 'We lie loudest when we lie to ourselves.' *Anon.*

The Enemies of Conviction

The two major enemies of conviction are apathy and inertia. The word 'apathy' itself derives from the Greek, and means 'no feelings'. Let me tell you a little story. A churchman once asked a famous actor: 'Why is it that I, a preacher, can only fill my church once a week even though I speak great religious truths, while you can fill a theatre every night even though you speak only fiction.' The famous actor replied: 'It's quite easy, Reverend, you see you speak truth as if it were fiction, while I speak fiction as if it were truth.' The moral is quite simple. A half-hearted manner born of apathy and inertia will never fill churches or theatres, win votes, sell products, or generally convince people. Before we can hope to convince others we must first of all convince ourselves. For we become eloquent only when we speak forcefully, courageously and sincerely on behalf of our ideals and convictions.

Another enemy of conviction is a *fear* of others who hold different views to ours and how these people might affect us and our life. There is also the enemy of undue conformity. For while a certain amount of conformity is necessary for our very survival, there is the danger that we might not take any initiative because of the fear of going out on a limb and of appearing to say the 'wrong' thing in the eyes of others. This is where having the courage of our convictions, as we have seen, comes into play.

Your deeply held convictions may occasionally go through a 'dark night of the soul'. Whenever you achieve success, you feel good. It peps up your confidence in yourself and your convictions. But when your convictions are under fire, from internal doubts or from outside, you can feel terribly down — psychologically 'spat upon'. It is at these times that you need some injections of hope, confidence, and courage for the sake of your morale. At these times, if you re-read the previous section, 'Having the Courage of Your Convictions', you may find in it a little bit of the encouragement and inspiration you need.

Apropos of inspiration and conviction's dark night of the soul, one example of how people persevere at these times of stress is by repeating to themselves a motto that sums up their conviction whether it be a business, political, or religious motto. One example that comes to mind is the Christian Church's practice in times of opposition of repeating and receiving hope from the words of Christ: 'Behold I am with you all days even until the end of the world.' Another example is that of the Civil Rights Movement's 'We Shall Overcome'.

The positive way of looking at your occasional failures or regressions is to regard them as learning opportunites to progress even further and to adjust better to life. The question to ask is: What went wrong and why? Then re-dedicate yourself to your convictions. Above all never identify with any failures and say, 'I am a failure.' A failure is not you. It is a single incident. Just admit it, learn from it, and say: 'Okay, next business.'

Inoculating Your Beliefs

Your convictions, beliefs, the things about which you feel most certain will be questioned from time to time. This shouldn't worry you if your beliefs are rationally held. In fact it is not a bad thing to hear objections to your convictions. Why wait, however, for the verbal or written attack? Why not act as a devil's advocate and pretend you are another party attacking your beliefs? Then be yourself and verbally defend your beliefs. This practice helps you to 'inoculate' them against real attack, highlights where your beliefs might be vulnerable and where they might need clarification or modification, and it also prepares you to defend them with conviction.

Another form of inoculation is the reading of books and newspapers which represent views contrary to your own. The committed Christian, for example, might read what Nietzsche, Bertrand Russell, and Karl Marx had to say about Christianity.

So, look closely at your convictions and reassess them from time to time. Ask yourself: Why do I hold these convictions? For example, why do I believe (or not believe) in God, in trade unionism, in the work I do, in the United Nations, in nuclear disarmament, and so on? How did I come to have my convictions? How valid are they in the light of experience and changing times? What are the major arguments for and against my convictions? Are my convictions worth defending? Do they need modifying?

Finally, if you feel a conviction does not stand up to the inoculation test, should you have it all all? Besides, if you don't examine your beliefs critically from time to time, you may lose sight of why you hold them in the first place. Remember, inoculation strengthens.

The Integrity of Others

As you express your convictions, beliefs, values, bear in mind the virtue of tolerance. This implies that you have a respect for the integrity of others, that you are prepared to listen to people holding views contrary to those held by you, and that you are prepared to respect their right and freedom to hold these views. A belief in tolerance can also lead us to the conclusion that everything in life is not necessarily black or white. In some instances, a degree of ambiguity will have to be acknowledged and tolerated. The practical implementation of tolerance in daily living may require a degree of compromise if people are to live in peace and harmony.

But to what extent should we compromise our convictions? You will have to decide how strongly committed you are to your belief, principle, or conviction, bearing the 'black or white' blinkering factor and the ambiguity factor in mind. In general, people of conviction don't compromise on major principles that have been closely and rigorously thought out from all angles before being accepted. They are sometimes willing, however, to compromise on the details of working out a principle in order to facilitate the contrary convictions of others and in order to bring a meeting, problem, or whatever, to some kind of workable solution — a *modus vivendi.*

Your Conviction Workshop — A Daily Review

> *Each day I am reborn.*
> *Each day I must begin again.*
> — PABLO CASALS AT THE AGE OF 93

Ultimately, you are responsible for yourself and for your own life. You have to live that life as it comes at you daily and fill it with meaning which is relevant to you. Convictions, as we have seen, can make this possible. In concluding this chapter, let us now consider the idea of having your own personal 'Conviction Workshop' in which you make a daily review of how you lived up to your convictions. Here is a simple and practical exercise which you might find useful. The principle behind it is — the more we reflect, the more we develop. The exercise consists of looking back over the main activities of your day, reflecting on these and seeing how your activities have, or have not, matched up to your convictions, and then, based on your findings, resolving to act in a particular way from then on. It is what I call O R A : Observe — Reflect — Act.

In doing the exercise, be candid and honest with yourself, disconcerting though the revelations might be at times. Ask yourself: Did my actions and decisions accord with my established convictions? Asking this question can be a great reinforcement to your beliefs and values because you will be examining how your daily life is shaping up in accordance with your self-formulated convictions.

2   Inspiration in speech

We need men who can dream of things that never were, and ask why not.

— GEORGE BERNARD SHAW

In every communication situation there is a choice either to build up or to pull down. The language of inspirational speech is that of the build up. This is not easy to do because we may be afraid, unwilling, or simply unable to inspire people. In fact it is always easier to pull down than to build up. We usually come across inspiration in poetry, art, music, and religion — their inspirational purpose being to uplift the human spirit. Inspiration has, however, just as vital a part to play in everyday business, community, family and political life — spheres which need inspiration today perhaps more than ever before in history. Indeed the ability to use inspiring words is a necessary part of verbal leadership. Let us consider how speech — the subject of this book — can be made magical by inspiration.

There is a sense of wholeness about inspirational speech. A vision. . . an inner image. . . of a whole, as distinct from the parts that create the whole, that either is or is about to be. Let me illustrate this with a little inspirational story. Three men were working on a building site when they were approached by a person who, to them, was a stranger. The stranger asked them what they were doing. One of the men answered that he was carrying stones; another said that he was working for so much an hour; the third replied, 'I'm building a cathedral'. He, of course, was also carrying his stones, earning his money, but the vision of the whole was also there.

A sense of vision also enabled an inventor to see a steam engine in a kettle, an artist to see a David in a block of marble, a prophet to see a Saviour in the child, and a statesman to see a people in the multitude.

How does the inspired speaker build up the cathedral of his message in the hearts of his listeners? And when is an inspirational approach required? Let us look at the mechanics of inspirational speech.

When to Inspire

You will need an inspirational approach when you want to build up people's faith ('lift up your hearts') in something or in someone. You may want to inspire your listeners to do better, or more enthusiastically, things which, at the moment, they are doing in a half-hearted manner. Or, you may want your listeners (and yourself) to renew flagging spirits and to keep up the 'struggle'. You may want to present an imaginative vision of what 'can be'.

The following speech occasions will generally require an inspirational approach:

Political, athletic and sales rallies
Addresses of welcome
Pep talks
Sermons
Addresses of tribute (memorial services,
anniversaries, re-unions, graduations)
Keynote addresses at conventions and conferences
Commencement addresses, inaugurations,
beginning of term speeches
Ceremonial speeches

John F. Kennedy's famous inaugural address as President of the U.S.A., while being informative, was mainly inspirational. Remember the words. . . 'Ask not what your country can do for you, ask what you can do for your country.' Words such as these, if they originate in the depths of the heart, can touch deep emotions. Inspiration is not from lip to ear, but from heart to heart.

Kennedy's words had a profound effect at the time in inspiring thousands of young people to look into their hearts, and there was born a resurgence of charitable and voluntary service for the underprivileged throughout the world.

As one of the few really great speakers of the modern world, Kennedy also used an inspirational approach when he paid a visit to the country of his ancestors in 1963. In a speech to a joint sitting of Ireland's Dáil and Seanad on 28 June 1963, he said: '. . .For I sincerely believe that your future is as promising as your past is proud. . . .' He was apparently following instinctively or otherwise an approach best summed up in the words of Emerson: 'Treat men greatly and they will prove themselves great.' The inspirational talk, as used by Kennedy and great speakers, can help to bring about what psychologists call a 'self-fulfilling prophesy'.

The Positive or Negative Choice

Positive thinking plays a very important part in inspiration. As you look at yourself, observe the negative and the positive. You can develop either of them. Inspire yourself by keeping your mind filled with messages of encouragement, hope, vision. Avoid thoughts of defeatism, hopelessness, despair.

The Ace of Inspiration

Whenever you need to use an inspirational approach in communication, a simple formula worth considering is the following:

The A C E of Inspiration
(Achievements + Challenge + Encouragement)

In using ACE to inspire people you would praise their past achievements, present a concrete, exciting and rewarding challenge or goal towards which they should strive, and encourage them to have faith in themselves and in their ability to achieve that goal.

In using ACE to inspire yourself you would give yourself a pep talk on your past achievements, the opportunities and rewards you see in the challenge ahead, and you would then encourage yourself that you have the ability to bring about your vision of what can be.

Let us consider some ways in which you might reinforce the ACE to inspire yourself and others.

Inspiring Yourself

I had a Latin teacher who, quoting Aristotle, used to say: 'Nemo dat quod non habet' — 'No one gives what he hasn't got.' If you want to inspire others, you must be inspired yourself. Here are some suggestions which will help to reinforce your use of the ACE to inspire yourself.

Absorb Inspiration

Cultivate the habit of absorbing inspiration. Take an interest in the arts (music, visual art, poetry) as they can inspire us with great thoughts. Why not walk around an art gallery and observe the paintings that inspire you? In fact, become interested in all visual displays of achievement. Don't forget also, that the walls of your own home invite displays of artistic achievement. Listen to music that inspires you. Collect inspirational sayings and look at them from time to time. Seek out and absorb inspiration wherever *you* find it — in the mountains, at the sea, lakes, along country roads, etc. Mix with people who inspire you — 'Your best friend is he or she who brings out the best that is within you.' *Henry Ford.*

Explore New Ideas

Maintain your sense of curiosity. The French philosopher, Maurice Merleau-Ponty, referred to a sense of curiosity as 'wonder in the face of the world'. This wonder, or childlike curiosity, can help our minds to explore new ideas and can open for us the door to creativity.

Develop Creative Goals

Create some imaginative and exciting goals for yourself and think daily about these. This has been the practice of great thinkers and inventors — people like Sir Isaac Newton. When asked how he came to discover the Law of Gravity he replied: 'By thinking about it all the time.' Ideas that will help you further your goals are all around you — in the air, so to speak. Carry an 'ideas notebook' with you in order to capture the various fleeting insights and observations that cross your mind during the course of the day. Keeping this notebook allows your creative mind to know that you are in earnest, and this somehow or other makes inspiration more likely.

Appreciate Greatness

Consider: 'No sadder proof can be given by a man of his own littleness than disbelief in great men.' *Thomas Carlyle.* To inspire others and to inspire yourself you must be able to appreciate and believe in greatness and the concept of human possibility — not the power that exploits, but the sincere achievement of worthwhile human activities. Inspiration is not built on a cynical, mean or sneering attitude. Become familiar with greatness in science, art, literature, religion, politics. Read the biographies and autobiographies of great men and women. They contain stories of human ability, courage, vision, and are a rich source of inspiration to keep before your mind.

Be Positive

Whenever you undertake something, don't start out thinking defeat. Be positive from the outset. If you do become discouraged, don't forget that your own humming, whistling or singing are effective weapons against discouragement. Think also of the cathedral story at the beginning of this chapter. You have a vision of a whole which you are creating. Think of this vision and don't let any temporary discouragement about a detail of that whole upset you unduly.

Inspired living means that you are determined to be a success at something that deeply interests you. And remember: 'Success is constancy to purpose.' *Disraeli.*

Inspiring Others

In using the ACE to inspire others, you will reinforce your application of it if you yourself show enthusiasm and a strong personal commitment to the inspirational message — an 'it can be done' attitude.

The use of 'atmosphere builders' (where appropriate) can also help in getting an inspirational message across. Atmosphere builders are frequently used in rally-type meetings. They help to create feelings of dedication, joy, hope, optimism, courage. They can create a sense of magic. . . a feeling of electricity in the air. Some examples are: Flowers, decorations, banquets, music; Costumes (national, etc.) and uniforms; Flags and lighting effects; Visual displays of achievement; Processions and symbols; Ritual, slogans, chanting in chorus.

As regards tempo, the inspirational speaker projects a controlled and efficient sense of urgency. A lackadaisical, disorganised, too casual approach does not inspire. Finally, as you set out to inspire, remember that to have credibility your inspiration must be founded upon truth.

Opposition to Your Inspiration

The inspirational speaker will sometimes encounter opposition. And like the Don Quixote of Cervantes, he or she may be accused of tilting at windmills. On such occasions a speaker might retort by saying: 'Can you prove this won't work?' Or, 'Do you know, or can you suggest, a better way?' Regard any opposition as a challenge to your enthusiasm, and press ahead.

3 You as a persuader –
techniques of persuasion

Much outcry and little outcome.
— AESOP

The above quotation reflects the often heard cries of 'less talk and more action', 'action speaks louder than words', 'a committee is where minutes are kept but hours are lost'. Lengthy discussion is, of course, necessary on occasions and must never be discarded in our desire for instant action. But I do believe we would have more effective action if we were more persuasive in our jobs, on committees, in politics, or in any situation which demands a persuasive approach.

There is a number of factors which can help us in this regard — what can be called the requisites of persuasion. We shall be considering these factors in this chapter, but, first of all, who are the persuaders?

Who Are the Persuaders?

Do you tend to be a persuader or a non-persuader? The non-persuaders of this world are those who continually sit on the fence and watch the world go by without taking any real part in it. They are the perpetual hesitaters. They appear to have no firm views. The persuaders, on the other hand, are those who feel deeply about things, and have the following characteristics:

Persuaders have opinions and they state these
forcefully for or against proposals.

Persuaders take sides. They speak up for the 'good'
and speak out against the 'evil' as they see it.

Persuaders are enthusiastic about things. They have
a proverbial 'fire in the belly' about the subjects
that interest them. They let their enthusiasm show.

Persuaders don't repress their feelings. If deeply
moved by something, they are not afraid to let their

38

feelings show. They are people who mean and who feel what they say. They let their humanity come through.

Persuaders shape and influence their environment, yours, and mine.

The Power of Feelings

In reading about the subject of persuasion, you may come across references to what is called 'the appeal to the intellect' and 'the appeal to the emotions' as if these were two separate entities. I feel, however, that they should not be separated — man is a whole. In attempts at persuasion, there should be an appeal to both intellect and emotion simultaneously. Most people, whether they be salespeople, business executives, or politicians, who fail in the persuasion process, frequently do so because they present their data in a cold, detached, unemotional way and assume that it will persuade people. It doesn't. It is facts plus expressed feelings about those facts that move people and sway opinions. Feelings are contagious. You will influence the feelings of others if you show your own deep feeling and concern about the facts you are expressing — an 'I have something vital to tell you' attitude.

So, if you are concerned — angry — happy — enthusiastic — about your subject, let your feelings show. Don't just say, for example, 'I'm concerned about this proposal' but also, through expressing your feelings, reveal how deeply concerned you are. Get your feelings out on your sleeve where they can be seen and felt.

Having sorted out where your feelings stand on a particular topic, now build on this primary foundation by training yourself to ask what can be called the essential questions of any persuasion process.

The Essential Questions of Persuasion

No doubt you have often attended meetings where the speaker waffled on and on, and when you came away you hadn't a clue what he or she really wanted you to do or believe. Such speakers have failed to do any effective homework. They have failed to realise that where persuasion is concerned, any audience, or even a single individual answering a halldoor to a canvasser, will want to know the specific answers to all of these basic questions, namely:

What exactly do you want us to do?
Why should we do it?
How will we do it?
When will we do it?
Where will we do it?
Who do you want to do it?

The effective persuader analyses these questions prior to communicating his or her message.

Tackling the 'Why' of Persuasion

People generally are motivated to act only if they feel there is something in the persuasion process for them — a 'benefit'. If you want to persuade, you must ask yourself this essential and fundamental question: How will my cause, plan, proposal, product, or whatever, genuinely benefit my listeners? What exactly is in it for them? Will it help them, for example, to obtain any of the following: more money, profit, increased savings; better health and longevity; more success; increased security; more pleasure; more leisure; more justice; better recognition; a feeling of well-being for duty done; a sense of achievement; heaven or nirvana?

Having isolated the benefits, write them down. Then in your presentation, occasionally refer to these benefits. Use 'Transitions' or 'Benefit Phrases' to help bridge the gap between mentioning the action you desire and the benefits that will accrue to your listeners. Here are some examples:

Let me show you how our organisation will benefit from this proposal. . .
Let me share with you the reasons why we should fight this proposal. . .
This plan will be to our advantage, for example, we will. . .
Let me show you how this will . . . (cut your costs, etc.) . . .

Let me tell you how others have benefited from
this. . .
Let us have a look at what others have
achieved. . .

If you are arguing against a proposal, plan, idea, say how it
will adversely affect your listeners, for example (if relevant):
say how it will cost too much money; affect their health; destroy
the environment; give their community a bad name; take away
some of their rights; and so on as appropriate.

Stressing the Specifics of Persuasion

It is surprising the number of people who argue in favour of
something but fail to inform their listeners exactly what to do,
how they should do it, when, and where (as appropriate). They
fail to cover the specifics of persuasion. It is analogous to that
situation, well known to sales trainers, where the sales person
for some reason or other is afraid to close or 'clinch' the sale
and ask for the order. Let us look at these specifics in more
detail.

The What
Inform your listeners in specific terms exactly what you would
like them to do (or what they can do to help). In doing this,
simplify the action as much as possible. For example: 'What
we'd like you to say over the phone to prospective contributors
is written on this card'; 'We'd like you to write letters to your
local politicians'; 'We'd like you to sign the petition at the back
of the room'; 'We'd like you to sign a roster of duties to clean
up our neighbourhood'. If it is relevant, offer your listeners a
choice. However, it is better not to offer more than two ways of
doing what you would like done. Too many ways might
confuse the issue.

When informing your listeners of what you would like them
to do, slow up for the 'asking line'. This helps to focus
attention on it. Look at your audience when you speak the
'asking line' and if there seems to be any doubt, repeat the line.
If perhaps your audience cannot do what you ask, you might (if
relevant) suggest to them the next best course of action, which
you will already have worked out.

The When
Inform your listeners of when the action is required. The urgency and importance of doing it as soon as possible or even 'right now' might be stressed. . . perhaps encourage your listeners to start working on it immediately they go home from the meeting.

The How
Show your listeners how to perform the action (if necessary). This may involve illustrating practical methods of action, and asking them to rehearse the action.

The Where
Inform your listeners of the exact location of the desired action (if this is appropriate). Possibly supply a map.

The Who
Before setting out to persuade, a speaker should have identified who exactly he or she is trying to persuade — what marketing people call the 'target audience'. This ensures that a speaker is talking to and trying to persuade the right audience relevant to his or her message.

This aspect of the specifics of persuasion also implies that a speaker might (where appropriate) offer some motivation or encouragement to his or her listeners apropos of the task to be tackled. The speaker would in this instance mention his or her belief in the audience's ability to do this job effectively, collect these funds, gather in the votes, etc. (as appropriate). *The Who* can also imply (where relevant) the obtaining of a vocalised personal commitment to the desired task.

Sell Yourself First

In order to persuade others sincerely, it is essential that you sell yourself first on your message — proposal, plan, product — and on how it will genuinely benefit your listeners. Then, believing in your ability to persuade, set out to convince your listeners, basing your approach on the specific questions we have considered above. Before you do this, however, part of the process of selling your message to yourself is to do what I call a TIROF.

The TIROF Technique

This is a *Total Immersion Retreat on Feelings* about your message. In doing a TIROF, you get yourself into a 'feelings mood' about your subject and your audience prior to the speaking occasion. What you do is this. Close your eyes and visualise your audience. Then remind yourself of their needs and how your message will benefit those needs. Doing a TIROF will help to condition you psychologically for the task ahead, and enable your message to grow and develop in the solitude of your mind.

Ways of Reinforcing Persuasion

The Use of Slogans

Down through history, slogans have been used by skilful speakers (some of them unscrupulous demagogues) to influence the emotions of people. Slogans sometimes are a more effective way of achieving action than long discussions on the subtleties of doctrine. In such discussions, the desired action can sometimes get lost amid the rocks of academic detachment. Action slogans, on the other hand, can be easily learned and remembered and are frequently more easily accepted. When chanted or sung, they can be very effective tools in working up feelings to action and for putting heart into supporters of a cause. They become in effect 'wake-up words'. The chanting of a slogan can also reinforce belief. Where politics is concerned, the political slogan user might, however, be accused of being a rabble rousing demagogue by his opponents — and they might be right.

Here are some examples of slogans and chants used down through the ages:

(a) In the Acts of the Apostles, we read of the crowd crying out, 'Great is Diana of the Ephesians'.

(b) The Russian Revolution used the slogan 'All Power to the Soviets'.

(c) The French Revolution's 'Liberty, Fraternity, Equality'.

(d) The Civil Rights Movement's 'We Shall Overcome'.

(e) 'Romero. . . Romero. . . Remember Romero'.

(f) 'No More Hiroshima'.

(g) 'Your Country Needs You'.

(h) 'Citizens, what do we want . . . freedom'.

Directing Audience Thinking Towards Agreement

Sometimes a speaker might ask questions that set out to establish areas of agreement: 'We all want this project to be a success, don't we?' In using questions, it is usual for such a speaker to make a momentary pause to let his question sink in — and he hopes heads will nod in agreement. Some speakers start the nodding themselves as they ask the question.

A speaker might also direct the audience's thinking through positive suggestion. For example: 'I'm sure you'll agree that. . .'; 'As we all know. . .'; 'We come now to a most important consideration. . .'.

The Approach of Advertisers

Advertisers use reinforcers in the persuasion process. In using the power of suggestion, they employ the techniques of repetition, prestige linking, and confident assertion. The more frequently the product and its benefits are mentioned, the more readily the ensuing familiarity tends to breed acceptance. In prestige linking, the product is associated or linked with some prominent person or prestigious event. The message is also asserted in a confident manner.

People are often 'packaged' like products using the above approach. The most common example is the 'packaging' of politicians at election time. They are presented 'up front' as much as possible to create familiarity, and they are endorsed by prominent people in a confident manner.

Fundraising Dinners

Organisers of these events generally recognise that an audience is usually more receptive to appeals if it has been well fed, is relaxed, and is in a happy mood. Hence the use of charity plate dinners and receptions to raise funds for various organisations.

Personal Disclosure

Personal disclosure can play an important part in the persuasion process. For example, a speaker might say: 'Let me tell you why I feel as I do. . .'; 'Let me tell you the effect this story had on me. . .'; 'Let me share with you my ambitions (dreams, fears) for this proposal. . .'. Such disclosure can have the effect of creating a sympathetic bond between speaker and audience.

Reaction and the Hard-Sell

A speaker who sets out to persuade should bear in mind that an audience will usually react against any attempts at manipulation, the hard-sell, the over-use of superlatives and being talked down to. These attitudes on the part of a speaker will be considered by an audience as being outside their 'latitude of acceptance'. If a speaker's persuasion is founded upon facts which he believes and feels will truthfully benefit his listeners, he will be perceived as being a more credible speaker. In a sales situation, for example, the effective salesperson acts as a genuine consultant on the real needs of his or her customers or clients. This is far removed from hard-pressure selling.

Charismatic Persuasion

The word *charisma* comes from the Greek and means 'gift of divine grace'. In its popular usage, the term *charisma* is applied to people who are perceived by their admirers to possess outstanding qualities of personality. Where persuasion is concerned, charisma is reinforced if a person is also perceived to be highly competent (a leader in his or her field), credible, and trustworthy.

The German sociologist Max Weber (1864-1920) describes charisma as a form of authority which flows from a person's personality and ability to communicate, as distinct from authority derived solely from tradition, bureaucratic office, or law. According to Weber, charismatic people are usually those who have a sense of mission or vision, their message is geared to help people in distress in a particular situation, and they usually 'deliver the goods'. Their accredited level of charisma, he maintains, usually endures so long as things are working out well for the people being helped. In this way, charisma can be brittle. An example of this phenomenon is the case of Sir Winston Churchill whose charisma helped to bring his people successfully through the Second World War. The war needs of his country at the time powerfully evoked this quality in him. However, after the war, he was unable to lead his party to victory in the General Election of 1945. This failure was attributed by some commentators to his being out of touch with the real *social* needs of his people after the war.

In the realm of politics, therefore, the charismatic leader has the ability to clarify and reflect back, like a mirror, the expressed or unexpressed dreams, hopes, aspirations of constituents and to deliver action on them. When a political leader, on the other hand, is out of touch with these needs, commentators can cynically 'bury' such a leader with — 'There goes the crowd, I am its leader, I must follow.'

Where group leadership and action are concerned, any group of people can develop an overall feeling of 'group charisma' if they are working to a specific programme of action which they have spelt out for themselves in concrete, specific, and inspirational language, and if they are not afraid to express to one another their own dedication to the task in hand.

The world is cluttered with unfinished business in the form of projects that might have been successful, if only at the tide point someone's patience had turned to active impatience.

— ROBERT UPDEGRAFF

4 Humour in speech

Without a few minutes of laughter each day
I would go mad.
— ABRAHAM LINCOLN

People love to laugh. Indeed echoing the above quotation, the occasional burst of laughter during the day can give our often tired and serious minds a break from their troubles. Laughter can prevent us from going around the proverbial bend in a world where fingers may not at times be too far away from the doomsday buttons.

Indeed to be able to laugh at ourselves and to make others laugh is a human quality worth cultivating. A sense of humour can enable us to take life seriously enough when necessary, and to see the humorous side of life as well. It can help us to keep our cool on those occasions when the tempers of the people around us may be on fire and they may need a little dampening down.

And, although it is probably a cliché to say that a sense of humour can help us to make friends, it is nevertheless true that there are few things more effective for dissolving barriers between people than the joys of shared laughter. And, not to be forgotten, a sense of humour can make us an easier person to live with.

Occasions for Humour

It is helpful for anyone who regularly gives talks to have a collection of humorous anecdotes in their bag of tricks. Their use, however, whilst not essential, will generally depend on the subject matter, the audience, and the occasion. Indeed the use of humorous anecdotes on certain occasions is best avoided. Having said this, however, on most occasions they will be well received.

Well-told anecdotes are a very effective way of getting and holding the attention of your listeners in an entertaining way. This is especially so at the start of a long talk, when a bit of humour can help to relax your audience and yourself. Humour

47

can also be used to brighten up even the most dull of academic or technical subjects. Such subjects are often more easily understood if they are put across in an entertaining way. Anecdotes are especially welcome in after-dinner speaking. Audiences on such occasions are generally prepared to enjoy themselves. They are usually sympathetic and willing to laugh at the slightest indication of humour.

Building up Your Repertoire

Some people are gifted with a great memory for jokes, funny stories, and incidents. Their humour seems to come easily when the occasion warrants it, and they seem to have a natural ability to make people laugh. But for those of us who find it difficult to remember anecdotes or jokes, the remedy is to keep a proverbial 'little black book' in which to write down those humorous stories that appeal to us. We can then refer to this notebook from time to time to refresh our memory.

Joke books are another source of humour. Some of these have the jokes indexed under various subject headings. This makes it easier to find a relevant joke for most speaking occasions. Another useful acquisition is a book which lists annual events. In using such a book, we can link the appropriate day, week, or month into the general fabric of our talk. For example, 'As this is National Comedians' Day, I think we should have a look at the lighter side of this subject. . . .'

When you come across a joke or humorous anecdote that you like, consider studying it for its potential application to various speaking occasions. Take this old-fashioned joke as an example. The school inspector on one of his regular visits asked ten-year-old Peter, 'What is a statesman?' Peter quickly replied, 'A statesman is a man who goes about making speeches.' The inspector paused to think for a while and then said, 'Yes, that's a fair answer, but not quite correct. You see, Peter, I myself sometimes make speeches, but I am not a statesman. What do you have to say to that?' Peter thought for a while, grinned broadly, and said, 'Yes, I know you're not a statesman. You see, a statesman is a man who makes good speeches.'

This joke can have several applications. For example, it could be used to give a humorous definition of a statesman, or to refer to the witticisms of children. Another application could be its use in encouraging political canvassers to be statesmanlike in their doorstep talks, by preparing and rehearsing their message well. If you would like to imitate the professional speakers, comedians, and raconteurs, you could go as far as categorising, cross-indexing, and filing your jokes and anecdotes.

Finally, you might find that the standard jokes in your collection (from magazines or books) will need some editing at times in order to adapt them to suit your own style, vocabulary, personality, and the mood of the speaking occasion.

Editing Your Jokes

This involves making a few simple changes here and there in a standard joke. You might change a name, a few words, a character, the setting, or perhaps modify the action somewhat. For example, if you have a good standard joke whose theme would be relevant for a talk to business people, but the character is a doctor and the setting is a plane, you might consider turning the doctor into a managing director and changing the plane into a boardroom.

As you edit your stories and jokes for the spoken word, keep them simple and pare them down to the fewest words possible. This means that you give just the barest details which will be sufficient to build up to the climax of your punch line. The danger with long stories and jokes is that your listeners might race you to the punch line. The consequence might be that the essence of humour — the unexpected — would be lost.

With regard to good taste, the main rule is that your choice of humour should be suitable to your present audience. If you're in doubt — leave out. The safest joke will always be the one against yourself. If you do, however, involve some member of your audience in a joke, be sure in your own mind that he or she will appreciate it and be able to laugh with you.

Observation and Humour

The American comedian Jack Benny once said that truth is funnier than fiction. Building on this shrewd remark, you can develop your sense of humour by training yourself to observe the actual or potentially amusing side of everyday life. You might, for example, come across some explicit or implicit gem of humour in some of the following: news items; remarks overheard (children, people in queues or in lifts, etc.); something that went wrong during your day; some humorous misinterpretation or misunderstanding. However, as you consider giving expression to the humorous side of life, bear in mind the 'golden rule' — be in good taste.

Creativity in Humour

If you would like to create your own fictitious humour, you might consider using some of the techniques of the professional humorists. Very often their humour is derived from true observations to which they add their own imaginative touch. They might, for example: (1) Overstate or understate a situation; (2) Turn things around, such as reversing roles, the subject and object in a sentence, etc; (3) Create some incongruity by bringing together in close proximity unrelated words, events, characters; (4) Give a humorous twist to a word, a saying, or a definition.

Rehearsing Your Jokes

Taking a leaf from the professional comedian's book, it is advisable to rehearse your jokes or humorous anecdotes well, before incorporating them into a talk. Try them on your family or friends first, and if they don't 'get' the joke, drop it. Any joke that needs an explanation has failed. Rehearsal will also help you to perfect the punch line and the timing so that you will be all the more comfortable with your anecdote on the actual speaking occasion.

Delivery — Timing — Punch Line

Never read a joke or humorous anecdote to an audience. Tell them in your own words — they will sound much more natural and spontaneous. And as regards dialects, avoid using any with which you are not familiar. It will be far better to tell your story straight in your everyday voice — and the story will be just as funny.

As you tell your story or joke, try and visualise its characters in your mind's eye. In doing this, it will help to prepare your audience for your punch line if you show your own enjoyment in telling the joke. In this regard, however, it is interesting to observe that some professional comedians keep a 'poker face' when telling jokes. This, however, is part of their act and they have probably worked hard to perfect it. Remember also, to tell your joke slowly and distinctly (but not too slowly). Many jokes are lost or 'thrown away' because they are rushed or mumbled.

When you come to the all-important punch line, speak it a bit slower and somewhat louder than the lead-in. It is so easy to wreck a joke by saying the punch line much too fast in your desire to get it out. You can also spotlight your punch line by preceding it with a brief pause. Then after delivering the line, pause briefly again in order to let it have its full effect. Continue only when the laughter has died down. Another way of spotlighting the punch line in some jokes is by asking a question, such as: 'And do you know what he said? (Brief pause) He said, ''. . .'' '.

Finally, if your joke falls flat, don't look surprised. Just continue on with your prepared talk. Never explain the joke. Some comedians overcome the occasional failure by saying something such as, 'You were meant to laugh,' or 'You'll have to think about that one.'

Observing the Professionals

Observing the professional comedians (stage, radio, television) can give us some useful insights into their mastery of humour. For example, I have heard comedians use the following repartee with audiences: 'I know you're out there, I can hear you breathing'; 'How can you look so clean and laugh so dirty' (when there has been an unexpected laugh); 'It's a good one, write it down'.

I also heard a comedian being interviewed on television. He was asked: 'Are you a funny man at home?' He replied, 'No.' Then after a very brief pause, he came in with an 'off-the-cuff' punch line by saying, 'I never go home.' The great Irish writer and wit Oscar Wilde was a master of repartee — even on his deathbed. Disliking the wallpaper in the room, he is reported to have said, 'One of us must go.'

5 The assertive speaker

The greatest discovery of my generation is that human beings can alter their lives by altering their attitudes of mind.

— WILLIAM JAMES

In the chapter on conviction, I stressed the important role which convictions play in our lives. They give us an 'inner' power. The fundamental conviction, I pointed out, is the conviction we should have about ourselves, namely, 'I am a worthwhile person'. Being assertive means that you give expression inwardly and outwardly to this fundamental conviction. You would, for example, be guilty of self-neglect if, by your own fault, you let yourself fall into poor health through improper diet or lack of exercise. The outward expression of the fundamental conviction means that you are enthusiastic about yourself (your talents and abilities), that you stand up for your rights, and that you take charge of your own life. You recognise that your own needs are as important as the needs of other people.

The concept of 'power' and 'influence' is associated with being assertive. It is worth remembering that everyone has power — whether it is expressed power or potential power. Everyone has position power whether as human beings, parents, consumers, voters, trade union members, managers, citizens, etc.

In the following 'power formula', I am not talking about manipulative or aggressive power, that is, power which in various situations refuses to recognise the basic human rights of others and which sets out to violate, intimidate, or exploit those rights. What I am talking about is creative power or assertiveness — the power to change or do things in a non-manipulative way. It is also distinct from non-assertiveness or timidity, that is, where a person 'moves away' mentally, physically, and verbally from situations where they should act assertively. Here is how you might use your power in an assertive and creative way:

52

P = Position: Use whatever authority you have in your various positions. Demand your rights whenever necessary. For example, as a consumer, refuse to pay for poor quality or poor service.

O = Ownership: Ownership means taking control of your own life. Take ownership or responsibility for things (decisions, initiatives). As Emerson said: 'Do the thing and you will have the power.' Don't forget to be aware of your feelings and to maintain ownership of them. Don't deny them. For example, instead of saying, 'He made me feel bad,' say instead, 'I allowed myself to feel bad when I heard what he said.' And instead of saying, 'You're making me angry,' say, 'I'm getting angry with you.'

W = Worth: Know and value your own worth as a person. Avail of opportunities for personal growth and build on your strengths. Knowing your own worth also implies being able to accept compliments, and being able to cope with criticism. If you are truthfully criticised, accept it without becoming anxious or defensive.

E = Express: Speak up for yourself and your ideas. Express your own wants and feelings. And, if there is any difficulty in a particular situation, be calmly persistent in demanding your rights, and avoid being trapped by the counter statements of the manipulative party. Also remember, you don't always have to justify or give a reason for everything you do, or don't want to do. Finally, whenever you don't know the answer to a question, don't be afraid to 'come up front' and admit that you don't know.

R = Refuse: There are occasions when in our heart of hearts we know we should say *no* to certain requests, but often lack the courage to do so. Therefore, whenever you feel that you ought to say *no*, do so without feeling guilty.

Assertive role-playing techniques can also help you become more assertive. Think of some situation (work, social, home, etc.) where you would like to be more assertive. Then role play that situation in your mind and imagine yourself (mentally, physically and verbally) handling it in an assertive manner.

Many of the chapters in this book will also help you become a more assertive speaker. For example, the chapter on conviction helps you develop mental assertion. The chapter 'As Others See You' encourages you to let your body language communicate self-confidence and personal strength. 'Eye-Contact Skills' encourages you to look directly into the other person's eyes when talking to them. 'Developing Your Voice' stresses the importance of speaking in a firm, clear, and confident manner. The chapter on persuasion highlights the power of accepting ownership of your feelings, which also helps you to influence the feelings of others.

Finally, there is the classic anecdote about the ancient Greek philosopher Diogenes who was said to have made his home in a large tub. Diogenes was visited by Alexander the Great who was curious to see the philosopher. The great man asked Diogenes whether there was anything at all he could do for him. Diogenes replied: 'Yes, you can stand out of my light and let me see the sun.' Obviously an assertive speaker who had his priorities right — on this occasion at least.

6 Understanding logic – putting on your logical armour

He that will not reason is a bigot;
he that cannot reason is a fool;
and he that dares not reason is a slave.

— SIR WILLIAM DRUMMOND

A knowledge of Logic is an essential part of successful speaking. It helps us to analyse propaganda, think clearly, examine arguments to see whether they are sound or false, and generally to keep in touch with reality.

Logic can be defined as the science of reasoning. It examines the mental process by which we get from any data to a conclusion based on that data. If someone, for example, says our reasoning is or is not very sound, they would mean that we have or have not thought logically in forming our conclusion. So Logic is all about how we arrived at our conclusion. Let us consider some of the main areas of Logic and how they can sharpen our powers of reasoning.

The Syllogism

The syllogism is the major item in traditional Logic. Aristotle was the first to use the term, in about 350 B.C. The syllogism then became the accepted form of logical reasoning down the ages and was given a boost by St Thomas Aquinas in the thirteenth century. He used it, especially in his famous book on theology, the *Summa Theologica*, to lay down the logical lines of reasoning to be followed by the Church which, at that time, controlled most of education and culture in the western world. The classic form of the syllogism is as follows:

All men are mortal
I am a man
Therefore I am mortal

55

The logician in looking at the above syllogism would say that the conclusion ('I am mortal') is valid if we admit that the premisses — the first two statements or 'propositions' — are true and provided that the common terms in the premisses ('men' and 'man') have identical meanings. A valid argument is, therefore, one whose conclusion follows logically from the premisses. If someone affirms or agrees with our premisses in the above syllogism and denies our conclusion, he or she would be engaging in self-contradiction.

Note in the above example, that in the two statements of the premisses, something is affirmed of some other thing, for example, 'I am a man'. In the propositions of a syllogism something must be affirmed or denied of some other thing if it is to be considered a syllogism.

Why not practise reducing arguments you hear or read into their skeleton or syllogistic form? This will help you identify the speaker's or writer's underlying case, to get to the essence of the argument, and to judge how sound it is. When you have reduced the argument into the three basic steps of the syllogism, judge the soundness of the argument by asking yourself: Are the premisses true? How sound is the evidence supporting the premisses? Do these premisses support this conclusion? Does the conclusion follow from the premisses? Do any of the points or steps leading to the conclusion contradict one another?

Let us now consider in some detail the more common logical faults a speaker should avoid when arguing his or her case. A knowledge of these will help you detect the major fallacies that occur in arguments and speeches — a fallacy being an argument which seems to be valid, but in reality is not so.

Generalisation

The word 'all' and the word 'some' will sometimes appear in front of propositions in an argument, and sometimes neither will appear. For example, 'All Europeans are clever', 'Some Europeans are clever', 'Europeans are clever'. If the person says, 'Europeans are clever', you will have to ask does he mean 'all' are clever or just 'some' of them before you can enter into meaningful discussion with him.

The misuse of 'all', 'never', 'always', is known as generalisation. The speaker makes a sweeping statement. If I say, for example, 'Red-haired people are bad tempered', I am logically making a statement in which 'all' is implied but in reality only 'some' is true. Some red-haired people are, of course, bad tempered, but so also are some people of other hair colourings. Generalisation is common because some people are inclined to make their general statements based on insufficient data.

Generalisation is counteracted by putting the word 'all' in front of a person's statement and then showing that the statement is not true. One contrary instance can disprove a generalisation. However, your opponent might say 'That's the exception that proves the rule'. Your retort might be: 'Exceptions don't prove that a rule is true, but that it is false'. Apparently, according to textbooks on Logic, the word 'proves' originally had the meaning 'test'. So if you produce the one unfavourable instance, you have tested the rule and found it wanting.

Begging the Question

A person 'begs the question' when he assumes as true something which really requires to be proved. For example, 'women are better speakers than men'. This fallacy also crops up frequently in argumentation as the 'yes - no' answer bind. Here an opponent frames his question in such a way that whatever answer you give is damaging to your case. In Logic the classic example of this is, 'Have you stopped beating your wife?' The problem with this type of question (which demands a yes or no response) is that whether the husband answers 'yes' or 'no' he confesses to having beaten his wife.

The person 'begging the question' is inclined to use phrases such as: 'Everyone knows. . .'; 'You must admit that. . .'; 'You can't deny that. . .'; 'It's indisputable. . .'; 'All clear thinking people know. . .'.

A variation on 'begging the question' is where your opponent, in a subtle way, asks you a question that is framed in such a way that it suggests how you should answer. For example, 'Surely you accept that capital punishment prevents crime?'

Pseudo-Technical Jargon

This is where a person uses obscure technical jargon which generally confuses his listeners. This practice is sometimes used by pedantic speakers in order to give themselves an air of prestigious superiority. They capitalise on the fact that some people are easily impressed by the big words they don't understand. There are also some people who fear that asking a question might reveal their 'ignorance'. There is the classic example of the squire in *The Vicar of Wakefield* who asked his unsophisticated opponent the question: 'Whether do you judge the analytical investigation of the first part of my enthymem deficient secundum quoad or quoad minus?'

The retort to the 'pseudo-technical jargonist' is to say to him or her: 'I'm sorry but I don't understand what you mean. Can you explain it to me in simple words?' The chances are he probably doesn't understand his own obscurity.

Diversionary Tactics

The 'Red Herring' diversionary tactic refers to the introduction of any irrelevant issue which distracts attention away from the proper subject of the discussion or debate. Very often the 'Red Herring' is not too far removed from the original question, but it is usually a topic on which the person feels more comfortable or certain. Your retort to the use of this tactic is to point out the 'Red Herring' and to bring your opponent back to the original argument even though he might accuse you of evading his arguments.

As regards 'Red Herrings', it is interesting to note that in newspaper correspondence columns, the original issue is seldom concluded because so many of the succeeding writers introduce various 'Red Herrings' as the correspondence progresses.

'Wandering from the issue' is also very common in discussion. Ideally, as the discussion progresses, the speakers should stick to just one point or key issue at a time. If a person wanders to another point, call his attention back to the original point and possibly agree to discuss the new point later or concede it (if it is of little consequence) and then get back to the point at issue. The consequence of allowing someone to hop from issue to issue is that you may not be able to pin him down to a definite conclusion.

Another diversionary tactic is where a person pretends to answer a question, but instead answers some unasked question with which he feels more confident. Or, the person avoids answering the original question and instead poses one of his own.

Another type of diversionary tactic is where a person fighting for something, such as the eradication of some perceived evil (for example, poverty abroad), might be asked by an opponent to fight against what he, the opponent, perceives as a 'greater evil' (for example, poverty at home), and to forget about the 'lesser evil' (poverty abroad). The opponent, of course, conveniently forgets to offer recommendations on what to do about either evil. Both 'evils', you might retort, should be attacked, and ask him for his solution to what he perceives to be the greater evil.

The Appeal to Authority

Suppose you and I are arguing and I say about something — 'such and such is true'. You, however, question me regarding its truth and I say — 'It's true because X, who is an authority, says so.' In this instance, I would be guilty of the fallacy of 'arguing from mere authority'.

Strengthening an argument by quoting an 'authoritative source' can be valid, however, if based on solid facts. For example, an expert speaking on his particular subject can claim to speak with some authority, and we would more than likely accept his opinion even though we may not be able to fully understand his scientific reasoning. It is the appeal to authority for its own sake ('mere authority') that can be invalid. For example, if the same expert were to say 'speaking as a professor' and then commence to speak on something outside his chosen field, we would more than likely respect his views as an intelligent human being, but we should not start quoting him as an authority on the topic.

Speakers in using this tactic frequently try to bolster up their arguments by including remarks such as, 'History teaches us that. . .', '. . .(some big name past or present) would not agree with that', 'That view is old-fashioned' (an appeal to 'with-it-ness').

Some speakers give the impression that they have credentials which in fact they don't have. Ask them about their 'credentials' and their prestige collapses.

Rationalising

We are rationalising when we believe something first and then concoct an apparently rational set of reasons in support of our belief. The process is frequently used in support of harmless self-indulgence. For example, if my doctor has told me to lose weight, and I go on to indulge myself in overeating, I might rationalise away his advice for the present by saying: 'I'm going to enjoy myself. After all, a little of what you fancy does you good.'

Rationalisation, however, can have more sinister implications. For example, Germany after the First World War was demoralised and had its internal troubles of high unemployment and high inflation. When the Nazi Party came to power, it sought a scapegoat and decided to blame the Jewish people. Julius Streicher and later Goebbels were given the task of rationalising this conclusion by any and every means. History records for us the tragic results of this rationalisation.

The Mean and the Extremes

Most people like to think of their views as being a mean between two extremes. For this reason a speaker frequently sets out to convince his listeners that his position is a moderate one between two extremes which he identifies. Another speaker, for the sake of tactics might, however, start off his argument by presenting it in its most extreme form. When this is attacked by his opponents, he then puts forward a more moderate position.

Sometimes, however, there is no middle ground. In Logic the 'Law of Excluded Middle' states that there is no middle ground between contradictories. For example, 'A is either B or not B'. Or, 'A judge is either partial or impartial'. There are, however, degress in certain circumstances. For example, there are degrees of variation along the continuum between sane and insane, depending on a person's ability to adjust to his or her environment.

Clarifying Terms and Definitions

In most discussions there is a need from time to time to define and agree terms of reference. This is especially so when we are discussing abstract concepts ('Justice', 'Democracy', etc.). Failure to do this can lead people in the discussion to ending up sooner or later by arguing about different things.

The need for clarity may also dictate the asking of many questions during a discussion. For example, if a speaker says, 'This project is beneficial', you may need to ask, 'Beneficial to whom?' Or, if he says, 'We are exploring all avenues', you ask, 'Which avenues?' Clarity also demands that we give a frequently used term the same meaning throughout the discussion. This also means that we may need to stop a speaker from time to time to ask him what he means by a particular term, as he may have changed its meaning as he goes along.

Selectivity in Argumentation

It is a common tendency amongst speakers to select instances or facts favourable to their view ('Proof by Selection'), while they carefully ignore other instances or facts less favourable. In arguing against this, point out that they haven't got all the facts, then press home your own instances, and back these with all the evidence you possess.

Emotion in Argumentation

As human beings we seldom use facts in a purely emotionless way. The words we choose to describe certain facts will convey our underlying emotional attitude to those facts. There is the classic example of the word 'mongrel' which can convey derision for something which happens to be 'a dog of mixed breed'. Or, for example, someone who is absolutely dedicated to a particular creed will be called a 'person of faith' by his admirers or a 'bigot' by his opponents.

On a more sinister level, some soldiers in certain wars have justified their killing of innocent women and children by saying — 'They were enemy, not people.' Wars tend to encourage the use of over-emotionally charged words. 'Positive' words are usually applied to one side (for example, 'heroism', 'bravery') and 'negative' words to the other (for example, 'cruelty', 'mentality of the enemy').

Sometimes an opponent might try to provoke you to anger by being offensive, insolent, or by making fun of your cause. He may do this in the hope that you will exaggerate and argue less rationally. The secret is to 'keep your cool', but still present your argument as forcefully as you can.

Finally, in an argument, it pays to observe the emotional content of your opponent's words and to consider translating them into words that are less emotional.

Special Pleading

Here the speaker uses an argument against something or other in a selective context. At the same time, he carefully ignores the application of the underlying principle of that argument to his own personal situation. For example, the person who argues against unemployment assistance on the grounds that it destroys initiative, whilst he himself has a large unearned income which allows him to be a gentleman of leisure, would be guilty of special pleading. His argument, in fact, can be turned against himself.

The Logic of Implication

It is interesting to observe the logic of TV advertising. An advertisement might say, for example, that tests have shown that no other brand is stronger than Brand A. What this logically means, however, is that the other brands are probably no weaker or less effective than Brand A. The brands are probably equal in these dimensions. The suggestion, however, is that Brand A is the strongest.

Fallacies of Ambiguity

There are two types, namely, 'Equivocation' and 'Amphiboly'. The fallacy of equivocation would arise when a person uses a single word in two different senses.

A person speaks in an amphibolous way when a whole sentence uttered is ambiguous, even though each and every word in the sentence may not be ambiguous. There is a legend about the famous Oracle at Delphi in ancient Greece which says that the Oracle was never wrong. It, however, made its predictions in an amphibolous way. The predictions could always be taken in at least two different senses. So whichever event happened, the Oracle was correct. For example, during the conflict between the Greeks and the Persians, a Greek commander asked the Oracle who would emerge as the final victor. The Oracle — an inspired priest or priestess devotee of the god Apollo — is supposed to have replied: 'Apollo says that the Greeks the Persians shall subdue.' This answer leaves it unclear as to who shall be the victor.

Argumentum ad Hominem

'Argumentum ad Hominem' ('argument at the man') means an argument that is directed against the person, rather than against what the person says. For example: 'You can't believe what he says. He's a conservative.'

Argumentum ad Ignorantium

The fallacy of 'Argumentum ad Ignorantium' ('argument by ignorance') arises when a person argues that some statement must be true simply because there is no evidence to disprove it. Such an argument is fallacious because for it to be true we would also require positive evidence in favour of it.

Argumentum ad Misericordiam

This is an appeal to compassion independent of the facts of a case. For example, 'It's unlikely that he committed the crime because he is a devoted husband and father.' This statement is irrelevant as regards guilt in the strict sense, but the appeal might influence the punishment if the person is found guilty.

Ignoratio Elenchi

In the fallacy of 'Ignoratio Elenchi' ('irrelevant conclusion') a person starts out to prove something but ends up proving something entirely different. For example, if I set out to prove that the players on X team are better than those on Y team, but instead end up proving that X team players are wealthier, I am guilty of 'Irrelevant Conclusion'.

The Non Sequitur

A person is guilty of a 'Non Sequitur' ('it does not follow') if he has inferred a conclusion which does not logically follow, or have any logical connection with what has gone before (the premisses). For example, 'My friend John goes to the theatre a lot. He must be very clever.' He may be, but not simply because he often goes to the theatre.

Arguing in a Circle

The speaker is in effect saying 'P is true because of Q; Q is true because of P'. For example:

A says: X is a genius
B says: How do you know?
A says: Because 'Y' book says so
B says: But how do you know 'Y' is reliable?
A says: Because it was written by X who is a genius

Argument from Analogy

Sometimes in order to help him prove a point, or to make something more understandable, a speaker might introduce an analogy. This is something which has a likeness in certain respects to the point he is trying to prove or explain. The analogy is not usually complete, and frequently just one or two common characteristics are shared. For example, people of old in arguing the divine right of kings, would compare the relationship between a king and his subjects to that between a father and his children, or to that between God and His creatures, and claim for the king a similar authority.

Scientists and inventors often use analogies, that is, draw hints or clues from other fields of science, to help them in their investigations. Darwin, for example, in developing his theory of the survival of the fittest was led to his conclusion by considering Malthus' assertion that the population tended to press on the means of subsistence. Darwin, however, did not put forth his theory until he had made repeated observations under all manner of circumstances. After commencing his observations, he waited twenty-one years before publishing his views in *The Origin of Species* (1859).

The main thing to remember, where argument from analogy is concerned, is that the more numerous the points of likeness, the better and more relevant the analogy. However, an analogy in itself is not generally a sufficient proof for a conclusion, and the danger is that it might be pressed too far. You may need on occasion to point out the weakness of an analogy and to show where it falls down due to lack of similarity.

Extension

If your opponent defeats you on one trivial part of your argument, he might by tactical 'extension' try and lead listeners into believing that you are defeated on the whole question. The retort to this tactic is to concede the minor point and to argue for your overall position.

An opponent might also try to take some 'limited proposal' of yours and by 'extension' try to make it appear wider and more embracing than you intended. His hope would be to defeat you on the 'extension' and, by implication, lead listeners to believe that your 'limited proposal' has been defeated.

Another form of 'extension' is when a speaker asserts of the whole what he has assumed to be true of a part. For example, what might benefit a particular part of the city, might also, but need not necessarily, benefit the whole city.

Division

In the fallacy of 'division', a person asserts that what is true of some whole must be true of all its parts taken separately. For example, 'Europe is wealthy, therefore X country in Europe is wealthy.'

Inductive and Deductive Reasoning

Reasoning can be either inductive or deductive. Inductive reasoning is when you infer or draw out a general conclusion or principle from a number of particular instances you have observed. For example, 'Every instance of X I have observed has Y attribute, therefore all X's have Y (including those X's I have not yet seen).' Science uses the process of inductive reasoning to establish its laws, the scientist having carefully recorded his or her many experiments or observations on the phenomenon under as many conditions as possible before postulating a law.

In deductive reasoning, on the other hand, you would apply a general principle to some particular case, for example, inferring 'I am mortal' from the general statement 'All men are mortal'. You argue from the general to the particular.

Tautology

A tautology in effect says nothing new. For example, 'X is X'. Here the predicate contains nothing which was not already in the subject. While you cannot deny a tautology, you can, however, object to a person using it in an attempt to prove something.

The Certitude of Mathematics

Where human beings are concerned, it is not possible to have mathematical certitude in everything which concerns their behaviour. Be wary of global attempts to apply mathematical principles rigidly to every facet of human behaviour.

The Logic of the Mass Media

> *The medium is the massage.*
> — MARSHALL McLUHAN

The mass media, through a form of psychological massage, can powerfully influence our opinions by determining which events are given exposure. From a logical point of view, we should be aware of the following: (1) Some essential facts might be omitted in a report and, therefore, a fair account might not be given. The 'edited' analysis of the facts might be made to look as if it is complete. (2) Some weakness or a minor incident might be portrayed in an exaggerated fashion and thereby be made to appear as a major occurrence. (3) A radio or TV presenter's opening remarks might bias the rest of a discussion. Ideally, a brief, accurate, and balanced outline of the facts should be given. (4) An interviewer might interrupt someone answering a question before that person has sufficiently developed his or her point. (5) The term 'well-informed sources' might be used to cover up anonymous rumours. (6) Loaded words might be used to label people. For example, the terms 'progressive', 'reactionary', 'moderate', etc. might be loosely applied to certain people. The facts behind loaded words would need to be examined.

The Abuse of Statistics

There is an old saying, 'statistics can prove anything'. So whenever a person fires statistics at you, you might need to question that person on the significance of the statistics as follows — What methods were used in obtaining the statistic? What tests were used? How are terms in the statistic defined? How large was the sample? What controls were exercised over variables? What comparisons were made with any other significant factors? (For example, if it is the level of pollution in X city, what comparisons were made with other cities?)

Theory Versus Practice

In argumentation some people often decry theory in favour of practice. The theorist is often accused of being 'up in the air' whilst the practical person is said to have his or her feet on the ground. Where Logic is concerned, however, beware of drawing too rigid a distinction between theory and practice. Consider: 'Theory without practice is sterile; practice without theory is blind.' *Anon.*

The Appeal to Sentiment

A person might argue that 'such and such is true because people feel this way about it', or 'such and such is true because everyone believes it'. Majorities have been known to hold beliefs which were false. For example, a majority once believed that the world was flat.

Part Two

PREPARING TALKS AND SPEECHES

*If he, the speaker, understands his subject
ever so well but is ignorant of how to form
and polish his speech, he cannot express
himself even about what he does understand.*
— CICERO

7 Methods of speaking in public

The purpose of this chapter is to give an overview of the different methods of speaking in public. Ideally you should experiment with all the methods. You will find, however, that some will appeal to you more than others, depending on your style and personality. The occasion also frequently dictates the use of one particular method in preference to any other, as we shall see. Below, I indicate when each method might be used and I enumerate some of the broad advantages and disadvantages of each. The main methods are:

Speaking from an outline
Reading from a full script
Delivering a talk from memory
Speaking on the spur of the moment ('off the cuff' or impromptu)

The Outline Approach — Speaking Extempore

Speaking from an outline or brief notes is the most popular method of speaking in public. It is sometimes referred to as extemporaneous speaking because whilst the ideas are prepared, the exact words the speaker will use are left to the actual speech occasion itself.

In this method you would outline, usually on a postcard or postcards, the points you want to make. You would use single words, or just a few words, phrases, or symbols to represent your ideas. Your talk would, therefore, be prepared but it would neither be written out word for word nor memorised. Sometimes, however, you might include the actual words of the occasional full sentence if this is considered vital. The full words of a quotation might also be included if necessary. Then before the actual date of the meeting or speech occasion, you would practise speaking words to the outline of your ideas. The more you practise this speaking on your outline, the more fluent and certain your words become. However, the exact form of words in which you will embody your prepared ideas will be left to the actual moment of the speech occasion itself.

71

There are many advantages to be gained in using this method. It appears more spontaneous, conversational and direct than reading from fully written out notes. Constant practice of the method also helps you to develop a more fluent, natural, and personal style of speaking.

However, there are certain dangers to bear in mind. The great flexibility of this method and the room it allows for word spontaneity may tempt you into giving very little time to the actual preparation of your outline and to practising putting words to it. It may thus encourage you to rely too much on the inspiration of the moment with the possible dangers of drying up, straying away from the point, or being long-winded.

Reading from a Fully Written Out Script

There may be occasions when you will prefer, or have need, to write out your talk in full. This may especially apply to the longer talk. As a method it is frequently employed by speakers when presenting subject matter which requires very precise wording, such as: (1) Papers read at meetings of learned societies; (2) Presidential addresses and speeches which will be reported in full or in part in the media, trade press, or in professional publications; (3) Television and radio scripts; (4) Occasions that demand rigid protocol or procedure; (5) Serious announcements (too important to be left to the spur of the moment); (6) Standardised lectures read by the various lecturers (or tutors) of an organisation; (7) Business speeches which will need to be vetted beforehand by the chief executive of the company or firm.

The main advantages of this method are as follows. Writing imposes a discipline. It forces you to clarify your ideas on the subject as you chisel out your words. In this way it encourages exactness of language and it provides an opportunity for detailed correction.

Having a full script prepared gives confidence as it prevents the danger of drying up or the mind going blank. You know exactly what you are going to say, how you are going to say it, and how long it will take you to say it. It prevents rambling — a common tendency with many extemporaneous speakers.

With regard to the disadvantages, this method does not allow as much directness of contact with the audience as does the extemporaneous approach. If the script is not properly written (as detailed in the chapter 'The Script Speech'), this method can bring to the surface all that is heavy and laborious. And as most speakers have not been trained in the art of reading aloud, the delivery of the script is very often at a rapid rate in a monotonous voice.

Written Out in Full and Memorised

This method is sometimes used on special occasions of formal oratory (usually competitions) by a speaker who has an excellent memory and delivery. General de Gaulle is said to have been a frequent user of this method. In fact he seemed to act out many of his speeches unimpeded by notes. This method, however, and I must stress this point, is not generally recommended as it has many disadvantages for the ordinary speaker.

The danger of 'stalling' and of the 'mind going blank' is very likely to happen with the inexperienced speaker who uses this method. The speech itself will probably sound from the memory and not from the heart. If the memory is straining to remember the words, the delivery is in danger of losing freedom and directness and it can sound monotonous, stilted, and artificial to your audience. Apart from all of this, there is the amount of time required to memorise.

Impromptu Speaking

Impromptu (or 'off the cuff') speaking in the strict sense means speaking on the spur of the moment without having any time to prepare what you are going to say. It also applies to those situations where you are asked to speak at very short notice. On these occasions, however, you usually have a few minutes in which to get your thoughts together.

The subject of impromptu speaking is covered in more detail in the chapter 'The Impromptu Talk — Speaking on the Spur of the Moment'.

Memorising Ideas

A variation on the extemporaneous method would be to memorise the headings of your prepared outline and then to practise putting words to these. This can be a practical proposition especially if the talk is an exceptionally short one and you have a good memory.

8 How to prepare a talk

Order is Heaven's first law.
— ALEXANDER POPE

Where the subject of effective speaking is concerned, careful preparation of your talk is essential if you want to be a really good speaker. For if your talk is well prepared, with a definite aim in mind and related to your audience and the occasion, and if you are reasonably relaxed in your presentation, you will be a successful speaker.

Any talk you give must first of all be built on the solid rock of your own credibility as a speaker. As the philosopher Ludwig Wittgenstein said: 'Whereof one cannot speak, thereon one must be silent.' Let us examine your credentials to credibility.

Speaking with Credibility

Before you speak in public, whether on a course or on any other speaking occasion, you must have earned the right to speak. You will earn this right if you speak only on subjects or topics you have studied, experienced, and feel deeply about.

Your credentials established, you must add to them a sincere and enthusiastic desire to deliver a definite message that has been given some soul-searching thought. Thought is all important. Don't fall into the same trap as those speakers who, when asked to give a talk, adopt the attitude of 'I just stand up and say whatever comes into my head.' They are usually not very good speakers. They invariably mumble, repeat themselves, wander, and don't know when and how to stop.

Identify Your Purpose: General and Specific

It is important at the start of your preparation to make clear in your own mind the general purpose and the specific purpose of your talk. Knowing what you hope to achieve will make the whole process of preparation much easier.

Having regard to your *general* purpose, ask yourself: Do I mainly want to —

74

Inform my audience about something
Persuade them to do something
Entertain them with some humour
Inspire them
Convince them of the truth or falsity of something
Provoke them for some reason
Thank them for something

Note, however, that there may be an overlapping of the above general purposes in any one talk. One main purpose will, however, always predominate.

Knowing your general purpose, you now determine the *specific* purpose of your talk. This is 'getting the line' on whatever it is you wish to say. In doing this you try to identify, in a nutshell, the exact message or theme of your talk. You ask yourself, for example: What precise information do I want to impart? Or, in a talk whose general purpose is to persuade: What exactly do I want to persuade my audience to do?

Imagine, for example, that a person who missed your talk were to ask a friend who had been present what your talk was about. The friend, as regards a talk whose general purpose is to inform, might answer: 'He informed us that the company is doing well.' Or, 'He explained the three major causes of drug addiction.' If your talk had been one to persuade, the friend might say: 'He tried to persuade us to form a community policing group in order to help prevent crime on our streets.' The friend, in my examples, would be describing the specific purpose of your talk.

Having identified your specific purpose, write it out in the form of a simple, brief and easily understood sentence. Then as you prepare your talk, keep the specific purpose continually before your mind so that everything you say will be a development of it, come from it as from a source, and help to 'drive it home'. Observing this principle will help you to be selective in gathering any material that might be necessary. It will give you a sense of direction and prevent you from getting hopelessly lost and bogged down in possibly interesting but irrelevant reading or research.

Develop Your Purpose into a Creative Outline

Having identified both your general and specific purposes, the next step is to develop them into a talk in outline form. Producing an outline is the foundation stone of all speech-making. Even if you are going to produce a fully written out speech (as explained in the chapter 'The Script Speech'), you should always outline your speech beforehand. Outlining speeds up the process of speech-writing and helps to put logical order into your thoughts. Your outline will consist of —

An Introduction
A Body (Main Points and Subordinate Headings)
A Conclusion

As a general rule you can leave the preparation of your introduction and conclusion until after you have prepared your main points. It is possible, however, that whilst collecting material (if this is necessary) you may come across suitable items to act as an introduction or conclusion.

The most important thing in drafting your outline will be to get the 'real you' down on paper. You must become your own speech artist. I say this because your listeners will be mainly interested in what *you* have to say, your own original thoughts, your own deep feelings on the subject, not what someone else has said. If your talk is a mere repetition of other people's thoughts, it will lack that 'something', that personal touch, which is of the essence of effective speaking.

For this reason, you should always postpone any reading or research on your subject (if required) until after you have first thought out, developed, and written down in outline form your own personal views on the subject. You will then know, or have identified, those areas in which you might need to do some reading or research in order to reinforce your own ideas, fill in the background, seek out new facts, look up references, consult authorities, and possibly modify some of your views in the light of new evidence or facts.

Your speech originality will be helped by 'creative outlining' as follows. First of all, start a creative flow of ideas by looking at your specific purpose which you will have written down. Being aware of it creates a ripple effect of associated ideas in your mind.

Write these down as they occur to you. However, don't attempt to write out a full speech word for word. Just jot down in outline form the various ideas, reflections, past experiences, observations that occur to you about your subject. In jotting these down, use single words, short phrases or symbols, and perhaps an occasional full sentence to remind you of points you might make. At this stage, don't worry about order or whether any point is good or not so good. Evaluation comes later.

Putting Your Points in Order

After completing your creative flow, bring your logical mind to bear on your outline by putting your various points in order and by evaluating which points are the most effective and relevant in helping you put across your specific purpose. Discard those points which you consider superfluous. Also ask yourself: Does any point need reinforcement with more examples, illustrations, evidence?

Plan Your Take-Off and Landing

With the body of your speech well outlined, all systems are now go for preparing your opening and closing remarks. These critical parts of speech-making remind me of a plane journey. The take-off and the landing are for me, and I am sure for most people, anxious moments. However, if the speaker emulates the pilot and knows exactly how he or she is going to take off and land vis-a-vis their talk, they will have a high degree of confidence. It is wise, therefore, to write out your opening and closing remarks in full — and to stick to them. They are your safety line to confidence! If you have a good memory, you may decide to follow the practice of some speakers who memorise their opening and their concluding remarks.

There are many strong ways you can open and close a talk. A list of possible ways and also some general hints on openings and closings are given in the next two chapters.

Developing Your Options: Outline or Script

Once you have your full and final outline prepared with the speech body, introduction, and conclusion contained therein, a number of options is then open to you as to how you should proceed. Your main choices will be either to —

(a) Speak from your outline (extemporaneous speaking). In this method put your outline on a postcard(s). For ease of reading, write your headings in bold capitals and number the postcards. Practise speaking on your outline several times. The more you practise putting your own words to the headings, the more fluent your delivery becomes and the less you will be stuck for words on the actual speech occasion.

OR

(b) Write out your talk in full from your outline as detailed in the chapter 'The Script Speech'.

We have already seen the advantages and disadvantages of both of these methods in the chapter on 'Methods of Speaking in Public'.

Incubation and Creativity

Great speakers, artists, and inventors know the advantages of occasionally withdrawing from the concentrated creative effort in order to allow incubation or 'subconscious creativity' to take place. Indeed any work that requires a creative effort will be enhanced tremendously if we allow time for periods of incubation.

Incubation periods can be used to great effect whilst preparing the longer talk. You leave aside your conscious preparation from time to time in order to allow your subconscious mind to dwell on the theme. During these periods, your talk will be maturing in your subconscious and many new ideas will come to you. For the ideas and material gathered in your conscious preparation will be generating kindred ideas in your creative mind.

Many new ideas will come to you when least expected. For example, they may come to you while out walking, just before you go to sleep at night, or on waking in the morning. Whenever they do come, be sure to make a note of them at the time — otherwise they may escape from your consciousness forever.

There is another advantage in leaving your speech, or any creative effort, aside from time to time during preparation. Too much continuous concentration, as you re-draft and prune your creative effort, can sometimes lead to mental staleness and your effort might appear to your tired mind as nonsense. If this happens, leave your speech or talk aside for a while in order to regenerate your enthusiasm and creativity during an incubation period.

Consider Your Audience

The effective speaker tries to keep his or her finger on the pulse of the audience. So, in preparing your talk, keep your audience in mind. Close your eyes for a moment and mentally picture them. This is mentally getting to know them beforehand.

Ask yourself: What do I hope to achieve in terms of my audience? What is in my message for them? What advantages? Any disadvantages? What are their likely reasons for attending this meeting or event? What is their attitude likely to be (interested, indifferent, sceptical, hostile)? Can I forestall any misconceptions or objections to my subject? Have I related my ideas to their background, interests, knowledge, experience — to things which occupy their minds at this time? What questions are likely to be uppermost in their minds in relation to my subject? Have I incorporated a relevant anecdote, illustration, visual aid, or statistic with which they can identify?

Consider Audience Participation

If appropriate to the occasion, you might ask yourself how you can achieve some audience participation, for example, asking the audience to write down something, perform some action, think out some problem with you, asking how many have read something or other, etc. Remember, however, that when you ask your audience to do something, always explain what the participation is meant to achieve or prove. You should also thank them for their participation and comment on how well they have performed. If a solo participant, however, does not do so well in an individual task, cover up for him and apologise for putting him 'on the spot'. Try to get him back at his ease by asking him a simple question which diverts his attention away from his mistake and on receipt of some response (no matter how small), ask the audience for a big round of applause for him.

If your audience participation involves asking them to say something after you, you may need to request them to say it with you several times. Finally, always rehearse beforehand exactly what you would like your audience to do.

Aim for Brevity

> *Brevity is the best recommendation of speech*
> *whether in a senator or an orator.*
> — CICERO

In giving talks, you will usually have to make a selection from your fullness of knowledge and relate your selected points to your audience. In this regard, avoid trying to cover too much ground in your talk. Just take one or two angles or aspects of your subject and develop them adequately with an illustration or two, preferably from your own experience. Harold Macmillan has recounted how Lloyd George once gave him good advice when he was starting off his parliamentary career. The advice was: a young parliamentarian can afford to have just one point in his speech; a cabinet minister can have two; and a prime minister — well, possibly three.

Be Concrete

Your search for the right word should be a search for simplicity of expression — the most concrete, simple, and vivid way of putting across your message. Great orators have always been painstaking in their search for the right word or phrase. Here are some examples:

'Yesterday, December 7th, 1941 — a date which will live in infamy.' — President Franklin D. Roosevelt's Pearl Harbour Speech, 8 December 1941.

'There is no finer investment for any community than putting milk into babies.' — Sir Winston Churchill, Radio Broadcast, 21 March 1943. Churchill was here graphically telling his listeners that the proper feeding of the next generation would ensure the nation's future.

'A kiss for my earthly mother . . .. Peace to you Poland, my Homeland . . .. Go home and kiss your babies goodnight.'— Pope John Paul II, in Poland, 1983.

'The hand that once picked cotton will now pick a President.' — Rev Jesse Jackson, in a speech to supporters in New York, April 1984.

Finally, as regards brevity, simplicity, and clarity, see the chapter 'A Masterpiece of Simplicity and Brevity'.

'Sincerity' — How The Romans Saw It

Sincerity in your speaking is an essential requisite if you are to have any lasting credibility. People sense deceit and once deceived never forget. The word sincerity comes from the Latin *sine cera* which means 'without wax'. Apparently in Roman days some of the sculptors in that city of oratory used to fill in the cracks and chinks of their marble statues with wax. Someone selling a really well-made and genuine piece of work would advertise his marble as being *sine cera*.

You are being sincere in your talk if you set out with no intention to deceive or to 'pull the wool over the eyes' of your listeners. You really mean what you say. When preparing your talk ask yourself: Am I really sincere about this? Do I really believe this? If you don't, leave it out.

Sincerity also means avoiding the temptation to exaggerate, over-dramatise, or to 'liven up' material to the point where the truth may become distorted. It also means that you avoid quoting statements and figures out of context.

9 How to open a talk

It is vitally important to have an effective Introduction or Exordium. For just as a good start is essential for the sprinter, your opening, if well handled, will get you off to a winning and confident start. In your Introduction, try and capture the attention of your listeners in the most interesting way relevant to the subject and the occasion, and as you plan your opening, remember to keep it short, simple, and to the point.

Don't spoil your opening by —

Beginning with an apology for your subject or for your inability to speak. Examples of apologetic introductions would be: 'I'm not much good at this sort of thing'; 'I won't keep you long' (they usually do); 'I haven't had time to prepare' (if so, such a speaker should not be on his feet); 'I'm not sure if you will be interested in my subject'.

Destroying your authority by mentally suggesting in any way whatsoever that you are going to give a poor talk.

Creating any expectations for your audience which the rest of your talk does not satisfy, for example, if you say, 'I will show you how to . . .' — make sure that you do.

Ways of Opening

Here are some simple yet effective ways of opening your talk or speech. Choose whichever is most relevant to your subject and the occasion.

The Personal Opening

Here you begin on a personal note by using any of the following: (1) Saying why you are interested in this particular subject; (2) Expressing your pleasure at being asked to speak, or why it is a pleasure for you to speak on this subject to this audience; (3) Introducing yourself (if not already well known) and perhaps explaining your special qualifications for speaking on this subject.

The Quotation Opening

. A striking quotation from poetry or prose, or a relevant extract from a book, magazine, or newspaper can be a very effective way of opening a talk. The quotation should be brief, well-spoken (slowly), and it should relate to the specific purpose of the talk. Example: 'Ladies and Gentlemen, Emerson once said that the right eloquence needs no bell to call the people together, and no constable to keep them. Let us consider the power of speech in a democratic society.'

The Story Opening

Here you relate a brief story or incident that helps to illustrate your theme, message, or moral. Indeed a well-told story can help to arouse curiosity and suspense for what is to follow. Your story might be a general one (from literature, history, etc.), or it might be some personal memorable event (pleasant or unpleasant). You might also consider using a transitional phrase from the story to the message, for example, 'Why am I telling you this story?' In relating your story, you might find it helpful to use the following format: what happened? where? when? how? who was involved? why did it happen?

The Explanatory / Exploratory Opening

Here you begin by using any of the following: (1) Defining some terms (for example, 'education' in a talk on some aspect of education); (2) Saying how you are going to develop your theme (especially suitable for the longer talk); (3) Giving some background information (for example, about the venue, the occasion, brief history of your subject); (4) Giving a preview of your talk (for example, 'Tonight I am going to talk on . . . for two reasons. Firstly because . . . Secondly, because . . .'); (5) Stating some general principle (for example, 'nature abhors a vacuum') and then applying it to your subject (perhaps some pressing social need calling out for action, for example 'the loneliness of old age'); (6) Posing a problem and then saying that you want to share with your audience some ways in which they, and you, can help solve the problem; (7) Stating your specific purpose, for example, 'Ladies and Gentlemen, the first essential with regard to education is that it must not be mass produced. Let me explain what I mean by this . . .' or, 'Tonight I'm going to show you how to relax and avoid tension.'

The Question Opening

There are two kinds of question opening. The first — the rhetorical — does not expect a reply, for example, 'What would you do if you suddenly lost your job? (Pause) Have you ever thought about this? Let me give you some hard facts about unemployment . . . .' The second type of question opening does expect a reply, for example, 'Ladies and Gentlemen, how many of you have ever . . .. Please raise your hands. Well, tonight I am going to talk about . . ..'

The Dramatic Opening

The use of some showmanship might be useful as an opening if you are the last speaker at a meeting and the audience is tired and you want to 'awaken' their interest. Showmanship, however, must be handled with care. An example would be tearing up your prepared script in front of your audience as you say, 'This is the speech I was going to give. However, let me not detain you. All I want to say in a few words is . . ..'

The Link of Unity Opening

In thinking about your audience, you may find that you share with them some common interest, view, belief, experience, circumstance, heritage, etc. This link of unity, or common bond, can then be used to open your talk.

Other ways of creating links of unity might be (where relevant): (1) To refer to local conditions (problems, achievements, etc.); (2) To introduce to the audience some important visitors who are present and who have a connection with the subject of your talk; (3) To say, 'We have here today visitors from . . . from . . . and from . . ..' Apart from their use in opening a talk, links of unity can also be used throughout a whole talk.

President John F. Kennedy used links of unity to great effect throughout his speaking career. This practice began when he came home from the Second World War and decided to run for Congress. One of his speeches at that time was to the *Gold Star Mothers*. His speech was not (according to witnesses) very successful — at first — because he was hemming and hawing, and it seemed as if he did not know how to end his speech. He went on and on. Then suddenly, as if inspired, he said, 'I know how you ladies feel. My mother also lost a son in the war.' This was a turning point for him, because, from then on, links of unity became one of the secrets of his successful speaking. For example, in a speech in Ireland in 1963, he said, 'I regret to say that no one has yet found any link between me and a great Irish patriot, Lord Edward Fitzgerald.'

The Topical Opening

Here you begin by referring to some current event (local, national, or international — serious or amusing) which illustrates your theme. Or, you might begin by referring to some striking statistic, for example, 'The World Health Organisation has stated that two-thirds of the world's population earns less than . . . a year. Let us consider to what extent our country is helping to relieve this situation . . ..'

The Vision Opening

Here you commence your talk by introducing your vision or dream of what can be — for your organisation, your country, your company, club, etc. The rest of the talk would then reveal how this vision might be brought about.

The Provocative / Controversial Opening

Here you open with some controversial or novel viewpoint, question or statement with the purpose of stimulating or provoking your audience into thinking about your subject. It would probably be one which runs counter to their beliefs and which would get some reaction from them.

The Visual Aid Opening

A visual aid opening is an effective way to catch and hold the attention of an audience. You might, for example, hold up a pen in giving a talk on the power of the written word, or hold up a photo of a starving person in making an appeal for charity, or refer to some striking words or statistic already written on a chart.

10 How to close a talk

The Close or Peroration of your talk, in one or two memorable sentences, should draw together and round-off the various points you have developed throughout your talk. It should emphasise your theme, sum up, bring audience interest to a climax, and help to motivate the desired response from your audience.

When and How to Stop

The King in *Alice in Wonderland* gave very good advice, which speakers can take to heart, when he said, 'Begin at the beginning, and go on till you come to the end, then stop.' Many otherwise good talks are ruined by unplanned, weak or long-drawn-out conclusions. And one of the most distressing things for an audience to observe is a speaker who, having failed to prepare his conclusion, starts to fumble as he looks in vain for some hospitable 'airport' at which to land his talk. Such a speaker brings the inevitable crash-landing upon himself, usually with a disastrous ending such as 'That's all I have to say.'

It is, therefore, vitally important, if you want to be an effective speaker, to plan your conclusion carefully word for word in advance. Write it out fully, then once you have decided on your conclusion, stick to it. Some nervous speakers, however, in perhaps being over-anxious to please, find it difficult to conclude. They go on, and on, and on. And some other speakers are tempted to continue beyond their prepared conclusion because they feel the atmosphere is friendly and the audience look as though they are enjoying the performance. This continuing-on can lead such a speaker into fruitless repetition, and his talk can become an anti-climax.

A wise rule to follow is one that is well known to professional stage-performers, namely, 'stop while your audience is still eager to have you continue.' These performers know that boredom for an audience can soon set in after the peak of popularity has been reached in a performance. Your audience will be happier if you leave them wanting more. I have often heard people complain when a speech was too long, but I have yet to hear anyone complain when a speech was too short.

However, whilst following the above advice, be careful that you don't end too abruptly. A certain feeling of anticipation, of drawing to a close, should be felt by both yourself and your audience, and shown to some extent in your voice. Then when you have expressed the last word of your conclusion, you should sit down, leave the platform, or do whatever else the occasion demands.

Don't Spoil Your Conclusion

There are certain things I would urge you to avoid in concluding your talk as they would take away from your 'Command of Message' and also spoil an otherwise good talk.

> Don't bring new points, facts, or ideas into your conclusion. Remember, no second speech.

> Don't use apologetic phrases. For example, 'I know I haven't explained everything as clearly as I should have, but. . ..' A speaker should never mentally or physically suggest the attitude of: 'Awful, wasn't it?' Or, 'I hope I haven't bored you.'

> Don't add such phrases as: 'I could talk on this for hours'; 'I hate to bore you with more details, but I might add in closing that. . ..'

> If you use the words 'In conclusion. . .', make sure that you do conclude.

Ways of Closing

Here are some ways to help you plan an effective close to your speech or talk. Choose the most relevant, for your subject, your audience, and the occasion.

The Summary Close

This conclusion is especially suitable for the longer talk or speech. It consists of giving a summary of your main points, for example, '. . .And so, we have been considering the advantages

of a liberal education. We have seen (1). . . (2). . . (3). . .
These, therefore, are the reasons why we must prevent liberal
education from being submerged in a technological age.'
Summaries can also be used throughout an entire speech at
strategic stages as the speech proceeds.

Another summary technique is that of repeating the main
theme (or a minor theme) of a speech as a slogan, after some new
evidence or statement has been presented, for example,
'. . .And Brutus is an honourable man. . .'. This was said by
Mark Antony, more ironically each time he said it, in
Shakespeare's *Julius Caesar*, when he wanted to discredit Brutus
in the eyes of the people.

The Quotation Close

A short and apt quotation which sums up your theme can be a
very effective conclusion to a talk. The source of the quotation, if
known, should be mentioned. Here is an example of how a
master speaker used an apt quotation to close his talk:

> *And not by eastern windows only,*
> *When daylight comes, comes in the light;*
> *In front the sun climbs slow, how slowly:*
> *But westward, look, the land is bright!*

The above well-known lines from Longfellow were used by Sir
Winston Churchill in his famous 'Westward, Look, the Land is
Bright' speech, broadcast to the world, 27 April 1941. His speech
announced the forthcoming aid of the United States of America
during the darkest period of the Second World War.

A variation on the standard quotation close is the quotation
capping close. For example, if you began your talk with a
quotation, you might refer to that quotation at the end of your
talk and cap it with another quotation. Preachers sometimes
close their sermons by repeating their opening text.

The Story Close

Any brief story (serious or amusing), which is relevant to your
theme, can be an effective way of closing your talk.

The Participation Close

Here you end your talk by asking your audience to do

something in the here-and-now which is relevant to your theme. For example: (1) Having 'awakened' your audience to a realisation of the importance of your subject, you ask them for suggestions regarding what action should be taken on the matter; (2) Asking for a show of hands in support of your theme, proposed action, point of view; (3) Asking your audience to say a prayer with you; (4) Asking your audience to help you list the pros and cons of some question, or proposed course of action; (5) Saying that you have something to give your audience (gifts, brochures, etc.).

The Dramatic Close

In this close you dramatise your message. Here, for example, is how a Sales Manager ended a talk at a sales conference — 'I have placed ten pounds under each chair. Those of you who want it, please stand up now and look under your chair. . . Okay. . . The message is loud and clear — to obtain anything worthwhile in life, including sales, we have to get up and go.'

The Vision Close

You might conclude by mentioning your vision or dream of what can be. Here is how the late Dr Martin Luther King Jnr concluded his famous 'I have a dream' speech: 'I have a dream that some day on the red hills of Georgia, sons of former slaves and former slave owners will be able to sit down together at the table of brotherhood.'

In his stirring speech, Dr King spoke from his soul about the yearning of his black compatriots for equality of opportunity. His speech fired the heart of the Civil Rights Movement. In it he was helping his audience to visualise the effects which would come about if his fellow Americans would follow his vision.

It is interesting to note that whilst preparing his speech, he seriously considered omitting the famous 'I have a dream' sequence. He thought it might make his speech too long. Posterity, however, has benefited from his second thoughts on the matter.

The Appeal for Action Close

In this close, you mention the action you would like your audience to take. Your appeal for action should be specific, for example, '. . .We start our sponsored walk at 2 o'clock on next Sunday afternoon, the 15th of April, from. . . (venue). We then. . . We look forward to seeing you all there.'

In concluding a talk, a speaker might also suggest to the audience what alternative courses of action are open to them. General de Gaulle, for example, used this approach throughout his speeches during the May-June 1968 student and worker crisis in France, when he wanted the country to vote the Gaullist Government back into power with an overwhelming majority. His theme was: 'Anarchy or Stability — Totalitarianism or Democracy.' Note that the speaker's own choice is usually named last in the combination of choices offered.

The Climax Close

The climax close consists of a forceful restatement of your theme and it is usually accompanied by either: (1) A gradual increasing of the tempo, and raising the voice to a crescendo and then sitting down, or (2) a gradual lowering of the voice until it is almost a whisper (but still audible), and then sitting down. Here is how Robert Emmet (1778-1803) concluded his very moving and famous speech from the Dock of Dublin's Green Street Courthouse in 1803.

> . . .Let no man write my epitaph; for as no man who knows my motives dares now vindicate them, let not prejudice or ignorance asperse them. Let them and me rest in obscurity and peace. Let my tomb remain uninscribed and my memory in oblivion, until other times and other men can do justice to my character. When my country takes her place among the nations of the earth, then, and not till then, let my epitaph be written. I have done.

The Surprise Close

In the surprise close, you maintain some element of surprise throughout the talk and the impact or climax (of revealing something) comes in the final line.

The Question Close

Here you conclude by leaving a probing or challenging question in the minds of your audience. For example, 'In conclusion, let me leave you with this vital question. . . how can we make our educational system the best in the world?' If your talk commenced with a question, you might also consider ending the talk by repeating that question, together with your answer to it.

The Visual Aid Close

Here you might write, for example, three or four words on a chalkboard or flipchart which would serve as a visual summing-up and reminder of the theme of your talk (for example, saying 'On the evidence I have presented to you, there can only be one conclusion. . .' as you then write *More Calls mean More Sales*). Or, you might introduce an object (the subject of your talk) which you have been hinting at, but have kept concealed up till then.

11   The script speech

I was watching a TV news programme recently in which an international conference was featured. The camera focused in on the notes of one of the speakers. He had hundreds of words closely written on the page which was as full as any page in a magazine article or book. In addition, he read in a 'reader's tone' and hardly looked at his audience. I was not surprised to see him verbally stumble several times as he lost his place in the jungle of words.

The approach of this speaker is not uncommon. Many speakers who read their speeches, unfortunately do so from closely written scripts. It is, however, next to impossible to read a mass of small print and at the same time give an effective speech. You can, of course, have your notes as detailed as you like, but how you organise them is important if you wish to use this method successfully.

Preparing Your Script

Here are some hints to help you avoid falling into the same trap as did our friend in the opening story.

Use an Oral Style

As you write the first draft of your speech from your outline, try for an oral rather than a written essay-type style. Remember that to develop a spoken style, you must speak while you write. Your tongue is the best guide in this regard. So test your sentences by saying them aloud as you write and ask yourself: Is this stilted? Is it conversational, easy to say and easy to understand at a first hearing? Keep your words simple and your sentences short (avoiding long dependent clauses). Ask a few questions in your script such as: Who? What? Why? How? When? Where? For example, you might ask your audience a rhetorical question such as, 'You might ask me what proof have I for this statement?'

Avoid tongue twisters and words you might have difficulty in pronouncing properly. Finally, in striving for your conversational approach, use contractions where appropriate, such as, 'I'd', 'We're', 'Don't'.

Space Your Ideas

As you write or type your speech, leave wide spaces so that, later on, you can insert any corrections or after-thoughts as appropriate. Typing should be in large size type, in double or treble spacing. Leave wide blank margins at the top and on the left hand side of each page. These margins are useful for putting in timing notes during rehearsal and for other self-directions.

Paragraphs and Pauses

For ease of delivery use short paragraphs with big gaps in between each one. This psychologically prepares you to use pauses. Many speakers who write their notes closely together in long paragraphs are conditioning themselves to read quickly. They feel they must race to the end of that long paragraph.

In using the principle of short paragraphs, try to avoid carrying a sentence or a paragraph over from one page to the next — having to turn a page over in the middle of a thought can interrupt the smooth flow of your delivery.

Each page of your notes will, therefore, consist of a small number of short paragraphs. And on each of these pages you can indicate wherever a thought is continuing on from one paragraph to the next by ending your previous paragraph with three dots (. . .). Within each of your paragraphs you can also indicate your pauses by using three dots (. . .) or dashes (- - -) or bars (/). For example, 'What I want to say is this. . . we must strive for better results.' You can also highlight your key words and phrases by underlining them or by writing them out in different colours. All of these spacing techniques should make it easier to glance up at your audience without losing your place in the script.

Finally, don't be afraid to use plenty of paper and write only on one side of each page. You should also number each page. You will find heavier paper better than flimsy paper as it is less likely to rustle in the microphone or to take off in the open air if this is where you are speaking. Don't have the sheets fastened together whilst actually reading. It is better to move each page to one side as you finish with it.

Quotes

If you are quoting from some source or other, insert the actual words 'quote' and 'unquote' (or 'end of quote') in your script in order to make it clear that you are opening and closing a quotation. For example: Recently, Professor Smith said . . .Quote. . . 'We must improve our commitment to the Third World if these nations are to survive. . .' Unquote.

Pruning

Although pruning takes time, it pays dividends. Be ruthless in cutting out irrelevant material and unnecessary repetition. Severely edit your drafts until only the minimum essentials remain for getting your message across. And remember that whilst illustrations and anecdotes will help you put across your point, too many of them can bury your main idea. Avoid the long-winded anecdote.

Using Statistics and Technical Terms

Statistics are an essential part of the speaker's trade. Their too frequent use, however, can be very dry and lead the audience to 'switching off'. On the other hand, if you present them properly in a clear, brief, and understandable way, they can be a very valuable tool in illustrating a point.

In using statistics, bear the following in mind. (1) Relate your statistics as much as possible to the everyday experience of your audience, to things with which they are already familiar. (2) Speak them slowly in order to let them sink in. (3) Unless you are talking to a highly specialist audience, use approximate rounded figures. If the press are present, give the exact figure as well. (4) Help your listeners to 'see' your statistics. Members of an audience, for example, could be asked to stand or sit as appropriate to illustrate a statistic. (5) Write your statistics on a flip chart, overhead projector, or large card which you can hold up. (6) Finally, don't apologise for your statistics. Use them with confidence or not at all.

If you are using a technical term, explain it the first time you mention it and give a concrete example to illustrate its meaning. If you are mentioning the name of an organisation which is unfamiliar to your audience, give it its full title and consider writing the name out in full together with its abbreviation on a flip chart, overhead projector, or chalkboard.

Bringing the Script Alive — Using 'PERP'

You will bring your speech alive if you deliver it with a touch of variety in your speaking by using 'PERP' — Pause, Emphasis, Rate, and Pitch.

The Impact of the Pause

One of the most effective uses of the pause in the history of oratory is the following (I have marked in the pauses as the piece was delivered on the occasion):

> 'Never . . .(pause). . . in the
> field of human conflict . . .(pause). . .
> was so much . . .(pause). . .
> owed by so many . . .(longer pause). . . to so few.'

Here Churchill was paying tribute to the RAF for their endeavours during the Battle of Britain. He used the pause effectively to give his words the full significance he intended. Note how the longer pause comes before the most important words, namely, 'to so few'.

Churchill was indeed a master of the pause. In contrast, poor speakers, in their anxiety to talk on, fail to realise how effective the pause can be in emphasising and highlighting a particular word or phrase. Consider, therefore, using the pause whenever you want —

> To emphasise a point. Do this by pausing before and after the word or phrase. The 'after pause' allows time for the idea to sink in.
>
> To create suspense for what is to follow.
>
> To move to a change of pitch or increased emphasis.
>
> To show up transitions from one thought or mood to another. There should always be a definite break before beginning a new main heading. This allows time for the audience to adjust to the new train of thought.
>
> To bring back the straying attention of an audience. Hopefully you will have no need to do this. However, an

unexpected pause can be very effective.

To highlight your answer to a rhetorical question. For example, 'Why has the government taken very little action on the . . . problem? (Brief pause) Because it has not the imagination to encourage initiative.'

The length of your pause can vary from anything as short as the taking in of a breath, to as long as, say, five seconds. And this will depend on the importance of the word or phrase and how much you want to highlight it.

When you wish to move from one idea to another, the general rule regarding pause is: the closer the relationship of the ideas, the shorter the pause; the less close, the longer the pause. Finally, where the subject and occasion are concerned, serious subjects and 'dignified' occasions require more pauses and a generally slower rate of delivery.

Word Emphasis

We have seen how the effective use of the pause can help to emphasise words and phrases. The importance of individual words can also be highlighted by giving them particular attention. This is achieved by letting your voice linger on a certain word and by saying it with a little bit more force than you give to its surrounding partners. This technique brings out the full meaning of the important word and impresses it upon your listeners.

Churchill had a unique style of emphasising words. In fact he seemed to 'growl' out those words he wanted to emphasise. When preparing his speeches, he would use short sentences and short words as much as possible. He knew that the short words would enable him all the more to use his famous 'growl'.

In emphasising words, take care, however, to avoid an unrelieved and jerky 'hammering out' of too many words. For to do so would be to over-emphasise everything and the power of contrast would be lost.

Rate

The rate or speed at which you speak should be varied in order to keep the attention of your listeners. You should also avoid the two extremes — speaking at a constant slowness and, on the other hand, racing to the end like a galloping horse. The first extreme appears pompous, whilst the second appears nervous. The secret is sometimes to speed up and sometimes to slow down.

Here are some general rules as regards rate —

Slow up to emphasise your key words and 'punch lines'. Then resume the original pace.

Speed up on any 'asides' incorporated in your script or when speaking in parenthesis.

When you slow up, occasionally do so for the duration of a whole sentence or two. And speak a bit louder and as distinctly as possible.

The humorous speech will require a mainly fast rate of delivery, whilst the solemn occasion will require a mainly slow rate of delivery.

If you are making an impassioned appeal or a fiery denunciation, you will need to use a fast rate. If you are speaking in the open air, you may require a slower rate so that your voice may have the necessary time to carry to your listeners' ears.

Pitch

The pitch of your voice means how low or how high you speak. There are three main pitch levels open to you: high, low, medium. The medium pitch is, however, mainly used for most speaking occasions which do not require any out-of-the-ordinary expression of emotion. This then leaves you an opportunity for the occasional modification to a higher or lower pitch as the subject, the occasion, and the need for variety demand.

Here are some general hints —

Be careful that you don't allow your voice to fade away before the end of a sentence.

When you introduce a new point, raise your voice to a slightly higher pitch to generate some momentum.

Begin your speech on a medium pitch, and keep the higher pitch, if need be, for those moments when you have warmed to your theme or when you want to lead up to a climax.

In general, reserve the higher pitch for those parts of your speech where you might be demonstrating anger, annoyance, or excitement about something. The lower pitch is used when you want to invite your listeners to ponder something deeply with you. Make sure, however, when you drop your voice that it is still audible. Keep your listeners on their toes by speaking the occasional phrase quietly and by raising your voice slightly once or twice during your talk. Use a slightly lower pitch when speaking in parenthesis.

The Carrying Power of Your Voice

Effective speakers develop the quality of their voice in order to enhance its carrying power. This is particularly important when they have to speak without the assistance of a microphone.

If you are speaking without the aid of a microphone, bear the following in mind. Adjust the volume of your voice to suit the size of the room or hall. There is no need to shout, however, but it will help your voice carry if you 'throw' or direct it to the back row so that all can hear. Articulating your words will help your voice to carry. So also will proper breathing, as sound is carried on breath. It is important, therefore, not to run out of breath. In this regard, why not practise the breathing exercises given in the chapter 'Developing Your Voice'.

Rehearse Your Talk

Many speakers put a lot of preparation into their talks, but fail to rehearse speaking them out loud. Failure to do so means that they will in effect be hearing their speech out loud for the first time when they address their audience. And their voice will sound strange to them. Lack of rehearsal can also lead to stumbling over words, and misreading. Speakers should, therefore, take a leaf from the actor's book. Actors have several rehearsals and finally a dress rehearsal before the real event of opening night. They can truly say, 'it will be all right on the night', but only because of the sweat of rehearsal after rehearsal.

The more a speaker rehearses, the closer will the script and the speaker's personality fuse together into an appearance of naturalness and confidence. Familiarity with the script also enables the speaker to look up more when delivering the talk.

As you rehearse your talk, do so in a standing position using the principles of 'PERP'. And don't be afraid to use gesture. Ensure that your talk is phrased in such a way that it facilitates easy breathing. Test it for timing. And in this regard, don't forget that an audience will applaud your talk and hopefully laugh at your anecdotes. So allowances should be made for these when you time yourself.

12 The power of three

What I tell you three times is true.

— LEWIS CARROLL

The above quotation from *Hunting of the Snark* is not as silly as it might seem. For in the realm of speech and writing, the effective saying of a thing three times in special repetitive combinations can reinforce a message powerfully. It is what I call the 'Power of Three'. This technique will add greater force, emphasis, and conviction to what you are saying.

Here is how the technique might be applied to either arguing for or against a proposal — 'This is an admirable, realistic, and workable proposal.' Or, 'The cost would be massive, astronomical, prohibitive.'

Note how in the above examples the three key words describing the proposal are arranged in cumulative sequence. The words very often can mean the same thing but they have the force of repetition and verbal intensity. Whatever you feel is the strongest word should be placed last in the series and should be given a pronounced emphasis as you say it. A major reason for doing this is that sometimes, for some reason or other, an audience may not have heard or fully absorbed your first word.

You will often hear the 'Power of Three' applied to people and events. For example: 'Are our politicians incapable of coming up with nothing more visionary, constructive, and practicable?' And as applied to a possible event: 'A nuclear war would be horrific, disastrous, catastrophic.' Here is how it might apply to defining something: 'Education is a process of learning, unfolding, becoming.'

See how it has been used to emphasise facts in a crisp way:

In January 1981, President Jimmy Carter, in announcing the release of the American hostages who had been held in Teheran, said that they were 'Alive, well, and free.'

Caesar's famous, 'Veni, Vidi, Vici' ('I came, I saw, I conquered').

A newspaper report — 'The appointments to the Board were greeted with disenchantment, disappointment, and even amazement.'

In sentence form the 'Power of Three' can be most effective in building up a theme to a climax. For example, note in the following extract from a speech by a politician how he used three variations on the theme 'We shall succeed'. Here is what he is reported to have said: 'Your government, Mr Chairman, will not fail; we will succeed. The people will not lose; the people will win. The nation will not be dragged down; the nation will emerge triumphant.'

Churchill's famous phrase, 'I have nothing to offer but blood, toil, tears and sweat' has four key words. Not three. As an experiment I asked a number of people could they remember the rest of the quote after the words 'I have nothing to offer but. . ..' All of them left out one of the key words — usually the word 'toil'. Would Churchill's phrase have been better with just three key words, not four? What do you think? Which word should he have left out? The point I am making is that people remember a series of three, but seem to have difficulty beyond that number. Churchill, however, was a master of the 'Power of Three'. Note how in this other famous phrase, 'Never in the field of human conflict was so much owed by so many to so few', there are three key points, namely, *so much*, *so many*, and *so few*.

The great Irish orator, Daniel O'Connell (1775-1847), used the 'Power of Three' to great effect in the following impassioned speech when he spoke on the Repeal of the Union of Great Britain and Ireland. Note also the tremendous conviction his words portray.

I here protest in the name of my country and in the name of my God, against the unfounded and unjust Union. My proposition to Ireland is that the Union is not binding on her people. It is void in conscience and in principle, and as a matter of constitutional law, I attest these facts. Yes, I attest by everything that is sacred, without being profane, the truth of my assertions. There is no real Union between the two countries. . . .

I therefore proclaim the nullity of the Union. In the face of Europe I proclaim its nullity. In the face of France especially, I proclaim its nullity, and I proclaim its nullity in the face of the liberated States of America.

Finally, once you become aware of the 'Power of Three' you will find abundant examples of it all around you. It is a very effective tool to keep in mind as you pursue your speaking and writing endeavours.

13 A masterpiece of simplicity and brevity

The beautiful is the removal of all superfluity.
— MICHELANGELO

The great Michelangelo created his sculptured works of magnificent beauty using the raw material of marble. We can imagine him in his studio sweating hard to produce that simplicity of form he refers to in the opening quotation. The great speaker is also an artist. . . an artist who chisels out his master speech using the raw material of words which have been infused with his vision, conviction, and sense of artistry. In all of this, simplicity and brevity is the key. Indeed it can be said that the ability to condense great thoughts into the fewest words possible is an attribute of genius.

Such a genius was Abraham Lincoln. Let us consider his famous 'Gettysburg Oration' which is widely acclaimed as one of the greatest speeches of all time. This masterpiece of simplicity and brevity was delivered on 19 November 1863, when the war cemetery at Gettysburg was dedicated. One hundred and seventy thousand men had fought at Gettysburg in a crucial battle of the American Civil War. Seven thousand were killed in that battle.

> Fourscore and seven years ago, our fathers brought forth upon this continent a new nation, conceived in Liberty, and dedicated to the proposition that all men are created equal.
>
> Now we are engaged in a great civil war, testing whether that nation, or any nation so conceived and so dedicated, can long endure. We are met on a great battlefield of that war. We have come to dedicate a portion of that field as the final resting-place for those who here gave their lives that their nation might live.
>
> It is altogether fitting and proper that we should do this. But, in a larger sense, we cannot dedicate, we cannot

consecrate, we cannot hallow this ground. The brave men, living and dead, who struggled here, have consecrated it far above our power to add or detract. The world will little note, nor long remember, what we say here; but it can never forget what they did here. It is for us, the living, rather to be dedicated here to the unfinished work which they who fought here have thus far so nobly advanced. It is rather for us to be here dedicated to the great task remaining before us: that from these honoured dead we take increased devotion to that cause for which they here gave the last full measure of devotion; that we here highly resolve that these dead shall not have died in vain; that this nation shall, under God, have a new birth of freedom; and that government of the people, by the people, and for the people, shall not perish from the earth.

Reading Lincoln's speech, it is interesting to note that despite what he said about the world not remembering his address, the fact is that it is one of the most enduring speeches ever delivered. Indeed the battle, which would probably have been forgotten in the mists of time, is now remembered largely because of what Lincoln said on the occasion of the dedication of the cemetery.

The speech itself, one of the shortest masterpieces on record, has only ten sentences and two hundred and sixty-eight words, most of which are monosyllabic. And allowing for pauses, it takes approximately two-and-a-half to three minutes to deliver. Lincoln, in his search for the right word and phrase, spent days mulling his speech over and over in his mind. When it came to chiselling out the words themselves, he wrote and re-wrote the speech several times in order to get it as perfect as he could.

The theme of his speech is that the Civil War is about commitment to the ideal of democratic equality. The slave-owning, aristocratic South had challenged this ideal. Note how in his introduction he introduces his theme straight away. Then, after his ideas have been built up in an ascending scale to a climax, he ends his speech by repeating his theme ('All men are created equal') in a slightly different form in the now famous words, 'government of the people, by the people, and for the people'. In the body of his speech he eulogises the dead, justifies the sacrifice they made for the ideal, and comforts and inspires the living towards on-going commitment and effort to his theme of democratic freedom.

Finally, notice Lincoln's effective use of repetition and the 'Power of Three' several times throughout his speech, for example, 'We cannot dedicate, we cannot consecrate, we cannot hallow'.

14 Visual aids –
making talks come alive

A great orator turns his listeners' ears into eyes.
— AN ARABIAN PROVERB

A visual aid is something you show or display to your audience in order to emphasise, make clear, or reinforce the points in your talk. It is a powerful asset insofar as it helps you to capture and hold the attention of your audience. Its use also offers some relief or variety in your talk because it gets the eyes of the audience off you for a change.

Therefore, in preparing any talk, consider the possibility of incorporating or using some visual aid. These could embrace items such as the following: newspaper clippings; books; wall charts; models (static or working); slides; any relevant object; projectors. If you do decide to use a visual aid, the most obvious and primary hint is to check out its suitability and working order before you give the talk. Failure to do this might make it a hindrance rather than a help.

In general, the simpler the visual aid, the more effective it is. Written aids, for example, that are too detailed or crowded will only confuse. These should also, wherever possible, be written large enough to be seen by everyone in the audience. In this regard, test them out by going to the back of the room or hall and judge what impact they have on you. Are they readable and clearly visible? If they are not, consider dropping them altogether. If you have to apologise for a visual aid, should you be using it in the first place?

As you prepare your talk, carefully link in the visual aids and know exactly how and where you are going to use them. Practise bringing them into view. If the aid is an object or product, practise handling it. Then as you rehearse your talk, practise co-ordinating your words with your actual use of the visual aids, so that both you and they 'feel comfortable' together.

106

Exhibiting Objects

In general, exhibits should be kept completely out of sight, or at least covered up, until they are required. If they are constantly in sight, or if you introduce them before the right moment, they will lose their dramatic impact. When your exhibit has done its job, remove it from sight. You might decide, however, to put it on display or pass it around the audience after your talk so that those interested in learning more can study it in more detail.

If you are using a model, stand behind it as you talk and possibly use a pointer to point out its features. Make sure the model is high enough off the ground for all to see.

If you are holding up an object, make sure that it does not cover your face. Hold it just above shoulder level a short distance in front of you. As you talk, make sure you keep eye-contact with your audience — some speakers forget about their audience and carry on a dialogue with their visual aid.

Films and Slides

Don't use films merely to fill in a gap in your presentation or programme. They should be relevant to the theme. Try, if at all possible, to avoid showing a film immediately after lunch (the speaker's 'graveyard session'). Have your film threaded beforehand, check the focus, and adjust the tone and volume controls to suit the size of the room. Carefully dovetail your talk with the film.

If you are using slides, make sure they are in correct sequence and inserted properly. Test the slides and the focusing beforehand.

The Overhead Projector

An overhead projector has the great advantage that it does not require a darkened room. It enables you to face your audience as you speak, while at the same time you project prepared transparencies on to the screen behind you. Or you can write in the 'here and now' on the projector's acetate roll, by means of special pens, as you illustrate a point in your talk. You can also achieve 'progressive' disclosure of the points on your prepared transparencies by gradually moving a sheet of paper down the slide as you finish with each point.

Make sure the writing on your prepared slides is legible, preferably in block letters or typing. Don't have too much writing on each slide — three or four short lines would be sufficient. Consider letting your audience read the slide before you speak on it. Number your slides and number your notes correspondingly. It is advisable to have a spare projection bulb and also to know how to insert it.

Boards and Charts

When you use a chalkboard, it is usually more effective (unless you have perfect handwriting) to print in large block letters so that those at the back of the room can see. As you write, turn occasionally to your audience to address them. The amount of time you speak with your back to your audience should be kept to a minimum. Use coloured chalks and underline, circle, or use arrows to emphasise key words. Especially write down complicated data, any difficult words, and unfamiliar names. Some speakers, in order to create suspense, write down a phrase on the chalkboard and leave it standing there for all to see without referring to it until later in their talk. This can be quite effective. Finally, try and avoid talking to a chalkboard, stand to one side and use a pointer.

Felt and magnetic boards, such as those used for weather forecasts on TV, are an extension of the chalkboard idea. They are worth considering if you want to build up an illustration as your lecture or talk progresses.

If you are using prepared flip chart pages, you may need to bend up one corner of each page so that it can be turned easily. Here again you might consider using a pointer to focus audience attention on the chart. Another idea is to write reminder notes to yourself on the chart (in light pencil).

If you hand out a short document, it may be advisable to give your audience some brief time to read it before you guide them through it.

Part Three

DELIVERING TALKS
AND SPEECHES

*Speak the speech, I pray you, as I pronounc'd it to
you, trippingly on the tongue. . . Nor do not saw the
air too much with your hand, thus, but use all gently;
for in the very torrent, tempest, and, as I may say,
whirlwind of your passion, you must acquire and
beget a temperance that may give it smoothness . . . .*
— HAMLET'S ADVICE TO THE PLAYERS

15 This thing called confidence

Self-confidence is the first requisite to great undertakings.
— SAMUEL JOHNSON

When All Eyes Are upon You

When you speak in public, your voice is the only one heard at a particular moment in time and every eye in the audience is focused on you. You are the solo performer. It is a moment when you can feel very exposed — psychologically naked. However, if you can learn to accept this feeling, whether you are simply reading the minutes at a meeting or making a full speech to an audience, no matter how large, you are well on your way to building up your confidence. This is why courses in effective speaking give plenty of opportunities to participants to stand up and talk in front of an audience, thereby gradually building up a confident acceptance of that 'all eyes upon me' feeling.

This part of the book deals with what I call 'Command of Presence'. This means being in charge of yourself when you speak in public. You display or stage manage yourself to your best advantage. This ability is vital if you are to gain the confidence of your listeners. An audience is always impressed by the person who displays a relaxed self-control. In the following paragraphs, there are a number of practical hints which will help you to be more confident, relaxed and effective before an audience.

Beginner's Nerves — Fear of the Unknown

If you are a beginner to speaking in public, it is naturally an unknown situation for you, with all those terrible fears the unknown can conjure up. Having to give a talk becomes an 'emergency' situation — an ordeal. The bells in your system ring out 'fear. . .fear'. Because of this, your body, in order to cope

111

with the emergency, produces adrenalin which creates energy for the 'great' or difficult task ahead. Your body will try to work off this excessive energy in various ways, most of which are well known to anyone who has ever spoken in public: trembling and clammy hands; jerky voice; the mind going blank; palpitating heart; shaking knees; shivers down the spine; 'butterflies'; dry mouth and tongue.

Don't let a description of these symptoms put you off speaking in public. These reactions of your body are natural and normal and indeed have been felt by thousands of speakers in all speech situations. So you are not the only one. It will help you to realise that even experienced and competent speakers, singers, actors, etc. feel nervous at times.

Even the 'Greats' Felt Nervous

There is a lovely story told about the famous French actress Sarah Bernhardt. She confessed to a not very well-known supporting actress that she always felt nervous before making an entrance on to the stage. The other, somewhat scornfully, replied: 'What, you a great actress nervous. Me, I'm never nervous when I make an entrance.' To which the great actress replied: 'Ah, yes, my dear, but wait until you have some talent.'

Even talented statesmen have confessed to feeling nervous. Such outstanding speakers as Sir Winston Churchill and John F. Kennedy confessed to feeling nervous when facing an audience. Here is how one great speaker, David Lloyd George, summed up his initial experience: 'The first time I attempted to make a speech, I tell you I was in a state of misery. It is no figure of speech, but literally true, that my tongue clove to the roof of my mouth, and at first, I could hardly get out a word.'

Another example is Disraeli. Before his maiden speech in the House of Commons, 7 December 1837, he admitted that being so nervous, he would prefer to lead a cavalry charge than to face that august body of people. When he did deliver his speech, it was so poor that it was greeted with jeers and ridicule by his fellow parliamentarians. However, not daunted by this experience, as he resumed his seat, he is said to have muttered between his clenched teeth, 'You shall listen to me yet.' And they did.

The nervousness of great speakers usually results from their desire to perform well. They are not content with giving a mediocre performance which is often the result of a false confidence, lack of preparation, and a careless attitude. In facing up to their nervousness, however, the great speakers force themselves to face their audience. In so doing they triumph over their fears and gain greatly in personal development.

Like the great speakers, your nervousness will lessen once you have the courage to begin your talk. Then as you continue on into your talk, you will be able to make that adrenalin work positively for you if you channel it into the forceful delivery of your message. This will enable you to be a compelling and vital speaker. And you will find yourself enjoying the experience.

Controlling those 'Butterflies'

The following tips will help you control those butterflies in the pit of your stomach when facing an audience. You will have great fun teaching them how to fly in formation!

Psyche Yourself

First of all believe you can become a good speaker, and you will. Nothing can stop you. Believe you can contribute something positive to the occasion.

Prepare Well

If you put careful preparation into your talk, you will be much more confident and you will have gone a long way to banishing your fears of speaking in public. And, as mentioned earlier, speak only on subjects with which you are familiar. Nervousness is always overcome by sound preparation and rehearsal. And, oh yes, arrive in good time at the venue. If you have thought about your audience — their attitudes and background — whilst preparing your talk, you will feel that you already 'know' them before actually meeting them.

'Live' Your Message

Let your enthusiasm for your message overcome your nervousness. The word enthusiasm comes from the Greek 'En Theos' and means a spirit or god within. Your confidence will be enhanced if you immerse yourself totally in your message by practising 'TIROF' (see page 43).

Try and Relax Beforehand
    If at all possible, try to relax by lying down or putting up your feet for at least ten minutes before giving your talk. Go into a quiet room away from the hustle and bustle of the platform.

Practise 'Act-As-Though'
    Many American philosophers have taken an 'it can be done' approach in their inspirational writings. One of these, William James (1842-1910), has formulated the philosophy of 'act-as-though'. The basic tenet of this philosophy is to act as though you already had the thing you are seeking and it will soon be yours. As James says: 'So to feel brave, act as if you are brave.' Why not try this philosophy whenever you have to speak in public by acting purposely and with confidence.

Be En Rapport
    Be *en rapport* with your audience. Regard them as friends. Their main preoccupation will be just listening to you. Most audiences are not there to 'get at you'. The world famous contralto, Madame Schumann Heink, used to pause before each performance, shut her eyes, and say to herself: 'I love this audience. I love each person here, I will give them my very, very best.'

Physical Activity Can Help
    Any physical activity or movement with a purpose behind it will help you feel more at home when addressing an audience. You could, for example, adjust the microphone, arrange your notes on the speaker's stand, sip some water.

Control Your Approach
    Just as a pilot checks all the instruments and then moves the plane slowly on to the runway before take-off, so also should you 'control your approach' in relation to your talk. In helping to adjust yourself confidently to your surroundings, try the following:

Listen attentively to the speakers who precede you. If you become interested in what they are saying, you will in all probability forget your own nervousness.

If you are entering a hall, make a slow deliberate entrance. If you are already sitting, stand up in a controlled and confident manner. Then approach the speaker's stand with this confident air.

As the height of tension in a tension curve usually comes just before you are ready to speak, take some deep breaths before rising to speak. This technique helps to increase your supply of oxygen and steady your stomach muscles — the home of those butterflies.

Having been introduced by the Chairperson, pause for a moment before you begin your talk. Never talk into any welcoming applause. Enjoy the stillness after the applause — there's a lot of magic in it. The magic of expectation.

When the audience have become silent and attentive, acknowledge the Chairperson and begin your talk slowly for about a minute. Apart from helping your confidence, this has the added advantage of allowing time for your audience to tune into your accent and tone of voice. This is particularly important if your voice is one they are unaccustomed to hearing. As you begin to feel more at home in your surroundings, you can then move gradually to your normal speaking pace.

Keep a Clear Head

Whilst some speakers may be tempted to believe that a drop of alcohol (or perhaps two, or three, or more) may work wonders for those butterflies, the fact is that during your talk the effects of too much alcohol can be disastrous. This may not be so obvious to the speaker, but it certainly will be to the audience. Instead of witnessing a controlled performance, they will 'see' and hear those tipsy butterflies flying not in formation but all over the place in disarray. Being under the influence, the speaker may be tempted to repeat himself, stumble over words, drag out his talk, possibly offend, and generally ruin his talk and the occasion. It is always wise to know your safe intake and to drink accordingly.

Grasp the Challenge

If you do feel very nervous, realise that there is never any shame in such nervousness. The shame would be in refusing to grasp the challenge and the stimulus your nervousness presents.

16 As others see you

When people look at you, they learn a lot about you from the way you physically present yourself — the expression on your face and in your eyes, the way you move your body, use your hands, etc. In other words, people learn from the 'whole' of the person . . . not just from the voice alone. It is important, therefore, to remember that when you address an audience . . . your body is your greatest visual aid. Any movements you make must not be restless, but must be seen to exist against a background of calm — a 'relaxed alertness'. This chapter, therefore, deals with how you should present yourself to your best advantage when you address an audience.

Mannerisms — Style or Inhibitions?

You may be unaware of your physical mannerisms until someone points them out to you. For example, a friend might say, 'You have a tendency to cover your mouth with your hand when you speak.' Or, if you have seen a video playback of yourself speaking, you may have noticed some disconcerting physical mannerism such as fidgeting with your fingers.

Whilst mannerisms can hinder you from making a good impression, it is nevertheless true that with some people a certain physical or vocal mannerism can be very colourful and useful when projecting their personality to others. If you have one of these, retain it. You may be in good company. Sir Winston Churchill, for example, had difficulty in pronouncing the letter 's'. In his early speaking days this was apparently a source of frustration to him. However, towards his middle and old age, he seems to have mastered his frustration more than the impediment itself. Indeed in listening to records of his voice, one gets the impression that he may have unconsciously exploited the residual impediment to advantage in order to achieve his unique style of delivery. You should, therefore, become aware of your own mannerisms in speaking — any mannerism that does not contribute in a positive way, should be eliminated.

Taking a Look at Your Mannerisms

The main advice I would give regarding mannerisms is to avoid making nervous little movements. Listeners start paying attention to these and they can distract from your message. Mannerisms also use up some of that vital energy, already discussed in the chapter on confidence, that should be going into the enthusiastic delivery of your talk.

Here are some of the more common forms of mannerisms: excessive fidgeting such as continuously playing with chalk, biros, keys, etc.; the adjusting and re-adjusting of collar and tie or glasses; scratching movements; covering your mouth; stroking your hair; aimless walking, rocking back and forth on your heels, swaying; buttoning and unbuttoning your jacket. I am sure you can think of others.

You should also avoid excessive verbal mannerisms. For example: not finishing your sentences; continuous use of space fillers ('you know', 'sort of', 'you see'); and the hesitaters ('em', 'eh', 'anda'). The use of these verbal mannerisms are more than likely the result of a speaker's lack of preparation and concentration. Some speakers use them to gain time to think out what to say next. I would recommend preparation, of course, whenever possible, but if you must pause on some occasions to think of your ideas, let your pause be a silent one.

Should I Stand or Sit?

Whether you stand or sit will depend on your subject matter, the occasion, and the atmosphere you want to create. Sitting does induce a certain informality. On the other hand, it is sometimes easier to convey strong emotion and forceful speaking from a standing position. Standing also gives you a better view of the audience and vice versa.

Arms and Hands — Where To?

Generally, in ordinary conversation, we do not think very much about our hands. When it comes to speaking in front of a group, however, we can become very conscious of them — suddenly they feel big and awkward. The question of what to do with them is a fairly common problem for many speakers. The best advice I can give you is to say that, once you begin your talk, you should forget about them as much as possible. They will then be free for appropriate gestures. Also remember that your hands do not seem as awkward to your listeners as you might think they do.

Discover what I call the 'Home Base' for your hands. This means that during a talk you frequently put your hands into the hand position most comfortable for you. This could be any of the positions mentioned below. Try out all of these to see which suits you. Knowing your 'Home Base' will help you to appear more natural and at ease as you face your listeners. Here are the positions:

(1)   Let them hang easily, loosely, and relaxed at your sides. To achieve this ability, however, is difficult at first and it usually comes only with experience. A variation on this position is to hold your notes in one hand and let the other hand rest relaxed by your side, or in your pocket.

(2)   Grasp the speaker's stand. However, never slump over a stand as it will destroy your 'Command of Presence' and in tilting your chin up, slumping places a strain on the vocal cords. You might also consider grasping the back of a chair.

(3)   Clasp your hands behind your back, or in front of you.

Taking Root

With regard to positioning your feet, I would advise that you 'anchor' your feet in one spot before becoming involved in any moving about. For ease, balance, and comfort keep your legs as relaxed as possible with your heels fairly close together, and balance the weight of your body equally on both feet. Avoid rocking back and forth. If you wish to change your stance slightly, do so during a pause, not in mid-sentence — otherwise, if you are using a microphone, your voice might waft away from it.

Movement

Moving about is appropriate in demonstration type talks and in certain lectures (for example, moving to a new diagram). In general, move when you want to emphasise a point, or to high-light a transition in your talk from one point to the next. Such transitions should be accompanied by a pause before you begin the next point. Your movement, however, should always be made with a purpose in mind. Avoid pacing up and down, and restless swaying.

Using Your Notes

First of all, in relation to notes, they should be your own notes, unique to you, and stamped with your own individuality. Don't attempt to hide them or be ashamed of them. Read them whenever you must and quite openly. Your reading of notes is made all the easier if you have prepared them in such a way that they are quite legible, and spaced so that you can read them quickly and easily merely by glancing at them. As regards the setting out and reading of full notes (as distinct from using an outline), refer to the chapter 'The Script Speech'.

The Use of Gesture

Gesture is an essential part of communication. It may consist of a raised eyebrow, a shrug of the shoulders, a movement of the facial muscles and lips, a flashing of the eyes, or an intricate movement of the head, arms, hands. It should, however, be absolutely spontaneous and natural, arising from the irresistible impulse of the body's desire to be a partner in the act of communication. Indeed a speaker with a definite message to put across will usually discover that, when well into his talk, he will be automatically using gestures to drive home his points. But while gesture must never be forced, it can, however, be improved in practice sessions. A study of gesture will give 'gesture fluency' or a repertoire of gestures to have in reserve.

Some Basic Rules
(1) Use large plain-to-see gestures, not furtive ones. Make them fully decisive and not half-hearted. (2) It must be obvious what they mean and what they emphasise. (3) Identical gestures repeated over and over again become boring to watch. (4) Avoid restless gesture and fidgeting, as they distract. (5) Avoid routine air chopping, banging on the table, and stamping the feet. (6)

Use vigorous gestures when you want to arouse an active emotional response. (7) Don't end your gestures too quickly. It is very effective, in certain circumstances, to hold a gesture even right through a sentence.

Gesture Exercises

Try practising the following gestures and in doing so make them as expansive as possible. Become an 'actor' for a while and try putting words to the gestures.

(1) The clenched fist for emphasis. (2) The pointing forefinger for warning. (3) The outstretched open hands for appeal, or welcome. (4) Counting off points on the fingers. (5) Pointing with a full arm extended to some object or in some direction. (6) Outlining with the hands and arms. (7) Contrasting sizes and shapes. (8) Letting the face mimic an emotion (for example, anger). (9) Simulating some action such as throwing a cricket ball or swinging a golf club, and putting the whole body behind the action. (10) Describing a spiral staircase. (11) Cupping the hands behind the ears to indicate hearing. (12) Arms extended, palms showing to audience to indicate need for calm or quiet. (13) Striking the palm with the fist to indicate 'now is the time to act'. (14) The index finger raised upwards to emphasise a point. (15) The thumbs-up sign for victory. (16) Holding out hands and shrugging shoulders to indicate doubt. (17) The thumb and forefinger circle to indicate excellence.

Make a Psychological Contract

Whenever you speak to an audience make a prior psychological contract with yourself that you will regard them as a stimulus and an inspiration. Then in addition to this mental confidence, face them with the physical confidence we have been examining in this chapter.

17   Eye-contact skills

Great speakers and leaders, in all walks of life, use their eyes effectively when communicating. They really look at their listeners, not only on those occasions when they speak in public, but also in everyday conversation. They realise the importance of eye-contact. Indeed, books on 'Body Language' and 'Assertiveness Training' tell us that the ability to make and hold extended eye-contact is an indication of a powerful personality.

Such a personality was Bishop Fulton Sheen. I once heard him preach to a crowded congregation. As I surveyed the congregation, I asked myself why had so many come to see and listen to a lean and ascetic looking elderly man, when so many of the young and robust curates at the time were beginning their ministry preaching to near empty pews. Here is my answer.

I observed the bishop as he entered the church. Immediately, as if by some charismatic magic which his presence triggered off, everybody stood up, and the atmosphere was electrifying. In his preaching, this man showed a genuine desire to communicate. Communication was his life and for him his spiritual message was all important — even greater than his techniques of communication.

What impressed me most, however, was how Bishop Fulton Sheen used his eyes. As he spoke, I felt his eyes giving me personal attention several times during his sermon. Those eyes spoke to everyone present. Several times when he wanted to emphasise a point, he leaned forward, looked directly at his congregation, said nothing for a moment or two and allowed his eyes alone to speak.

Poor speakers, in comparison, do not look at their audience. They look beyond them with an apparently vacant expression in their eyes. Very often such speakers have also failed to prepare their talks adequately and frequently regard the occasion as an ordeal to be got through as quickly as possible.

Your audience deserves the courtesy of your eyes. Never ignore them. You will be ignoring your audience — and they in turn will ignore you — if you continually stare over their heads, or at the floor or ceiling, or at any point beyond them such as the opposite wall, or out the window. You should instead make a great effort to 'bring' your listeners into your talk by looking at them confidently. Each should feel your eyes talking to them from time to time in much the same way as I did on the occasion described above when Bishop Fulton Sheen was the star performer. If you fail to use your eyes, your audience will find it difficult to believe that your message is significant for them. Here are some hints to help you improve your eye-contact skills.

The Eye-Sweep

It is a physical impossibility to look at everyone in your audience at the same time. So the technique of the 'eye-sweep' is necessary. This enables you to talk to positively identified individuals and small groups in all parts of your audience, however large, throughout your talk. What you do is this. You let your eyes sweep round from person to person if addressing a small intimate group or from section to section if addressing a large group. With a large group, however, you will still, of course, pick out and talk to individuals from time to time. As you look at those people directly in front of you, those to the right and left, and those at the back of the room, remember that the movement of your eyes must be a gentle, steady movement. It should never be rapid, jerky, or furtive as if darting round the room looking for a quick exit.

When answering a question from a member of an audience, don't look at the questioner all the time. Look at him in the beginning and towards the end of your reply and occasionally in between. Eye-contact with all your audience creates a feeling of sharing the answer to the question.

The 'Eagle Eye' Technique

The eagle eye of the law knows the importance of eye-contact skills. A barrister, when he addresses a jury, frequently fixes his attention upon those individuals whom he thinks are facially displaying scepticism towards his arguments. This is based on the belief that to see the face reacting is to see the mind reacting. Whilst he does not forget the rest of the jury he, however, pays particular attention to the sceptics in an attempt to win them over with his persuasive arguments.

A variation on this technique is to pick out a friendly looking face in the audience, and then another and another, until you have built up a 'collection' of friendly faces. The danger to avoid, however, is that of staring at the one person all the time — fixing your eyes upon one member of your audience and appearing to address your whole talk to that person. Such a person would eventually feel embarrassed, lower his or her eyes, and begin to fidget.

Observe Danger Signals

Communication is a two-way process. For while you are speaking, your audience in turn are responding mentally and physically to what you are saying.

Observe to what extent they are fully hearing and assimilating your words. Are they displaying any danger signals? For example, do they look puzzled or bored? Are they yawning, coughing, fidgeting or even falling asleep? If you observe any of these signals whilst delivering a talk, speech, or lecture, you can make a quick decision as to what adjustments (additions or deletions) you will need to make as you deliver your prepared script. Of course, it can always happen that some members of the audience may have had a late night and so cannot prevent themselves from yawning. And, believe it or not, there are some people who claim that they hear better with their eyes closed.

Finally, remember that a pause can have the power of drawing listeners' attention back to you.

The Eyes as Loudspeakers

Whenever you are speaking without the aid of a microphone, remember that, as a general rule, wherever your eyes look, your voice will follow. So when you look towards those members of your audience in the last row of the room or hall, your voice will tend to follow the lead of your eyes. It also helps if you imagine that you are a fisherman casting your voice about thirty cms above the heads of the people in the last row. The practice of the exercises in the chapter 'Developing Your Voice' will also help you to project your voice well on speaking occasions.

The Eye Pause

As you pause in your talk, 'feel' and experience the pause with your eyes while they scan your audience. This is what is called the 'pregnant pause'. In this marvellous moment, your audience is communicating with you. You will receive a vibration of comprehension from them. A skilled master of this technique is the charismatic Pope John Paul II. It may be the actor's training in his past coming to the fore, added to his deep concern for his listeners. I remember hearing and seeing his very moving talk to the young people of Ireland in September 1979, when he said, 'Young People of Ireland, I . . . love. . . you.' And he then paused, looked deeply at his listeners, and let the pregnant pause take over. There followed a tumultuous applause, which he allowed to continue for several minutes. He was enjoying himself. The eye pause is a friend. Use it.

Mirrors of Meaning

The old saying 'The eyes are the mirrors of the soul' has much significance for the speaker. In ordinary conversational situations, if we briefly pause and observe the other person's eyes after we say something, we will see whether that person has understood, is interested or bored with what we have said.

Finally, the person to whom you are speaking will get more of your meaning if you encourage him or her to look directly at you. This is helped if you maintain eye-contact yourself with the person as you speak. Also remember this little key phrase whenever you are being introduced to someone . . . 'Shake hands — engage eyes'.

18 Coping with hecklers

Every sort of shouting is a transitory thing.
It is the grim silence of facts that remains.

Heckling takes place mainly at political meetings, or at any public meeting where controversial topics are discussed. It seldom happens during after-dinner speeches — if it does it is generally of a mild or jovial nature.

The British statesman Harold Macmillan was once well heckled at a mass political meeting. However, undaunted by the heckler, he replied: 'Give the man a big cheer. Heckling is a very old tradition and not sufficiently exercised.' Many speakers, however, fear the forceful heckler who sets out to destroy the confident manner of the speaker and to take him out of his stride. The heckler tries to achieve this by interjecting a teasing question or comment with the intention of making the audience laugh at the speaker or making the speaker lose his temper.

As a general rule, the speaker should not let the heckler get the better of him. He should face the challenge and try to turn the heckle to his advantage if he can. It will be a feather in his cap if he can achieve this! In dealing with hecklers you might consider the following techniques.

Techniques for Dealing with Hecklers

Ignore the Heckler
Here you ignore the heckler unless you happen to have some inspired reply ready to hand.

Appeal to the Audience for Sympathy
This might well be successful. However, the danger in doing so is that you might lose the full force of your confident manner and prestige.

Appeal to the Chairperson
It is usually the Chairperson's responsibility to act if heckling is getting out of control and turning to hooliganism, such as

deliberate and organised attempts aimed at preventing a person from speaking. The speaker can, if necessary, ask a hesitant Chairperson if he or she intends taking any action.

A lot of heckling, however, will be of a mild nature and will not be organised. Individual hecklers will be 'playing it by ear', depending on what the speaker says.

The Silent Treatment

In using this approach, you stop speaking, look at the heckler for a moment, and then continue your speech. You could also use this approach with the person who heckles you in a 'silent' way. For example, a member of the audience might open out a newspaper loudly and then proceed to read it. Or he might pretend to be asleep or engage in continuous yawning.

Answer the Heckler

Answer the heckler in an amusing or serious way. If he gives you an opening for a short and inspired answer, by all means do step in with your serious or humorous riposte. If you are heckled in the form of a relevant question you could say that you will be dealing with that point later on. If you decide to answer a long-winded heckle, you could summarise it and then answer it briefly.

The 'soft' approach in answering a heckler is to ask him a question even though you heard him the first time. . . 'What was that, Sir?' The use of 'Sir' indicates politeness and non-aggression on your part. This then gives you time to think up a reply (a prepared stand-by comment or an improvised one), or you may decide to continue.

Some Standard Heckles

There are some standard heckles that have been around for a long time. Here are some you should be aware of: Apart from the ever-popular use of 'Rubbish', there is 'Shame' (said slowly at the right moment); 'Good job someone's happy' (when the speaker has said how glad he is to be there); 'Your prosperity' (when the speaker has told his audience that a vote for him is a vote for prosperity); 'Now tell us a really funny story' (when the speaker has made a string of promises).

You should also be aware that there are certain phrases that lend themselves wide open to heckles. For example, 'We must not bury our heads in the sand', to which the heckler replies, 'You'd look better that way.'

Rescuing the Situation

If something unexpected happens while you are speaking, take care of it by mentally giving yourself the command 'rescue the situation'. Then take whatever action is necessary. For example, if there is an interruption (a waiter drops something), don't ignore what has happened, but instead pass a brief comment on it and continue. I heard an after-dinner speaker amusingly remark on such an occasion: 'I don't mind. In my business we're used to competition.'

There is also the amusing story of the political candidate who, when addressing a meeting, made a false step and fell off the platform. On climbing back on to the platform, he calmly said to his audience: 'It should be the duty of all good politicians to come down to the level of their audience.' And there is the speaker who, having to adjust the microphone, said, 'I have to adjust this for inflation.'

The Use of Conciliation

Whenever active opposition, heckling, or any unfavourable attitude to proposals is anticipated, the speaker might need to use a conciliatory approach. For example, Mark Antony in Shakespeare's *Julius Caesar* began his famous speech to the people with the words, '. . . I come to bury Caesar, not to praise him.' In using this approach, a speaker might:

(1) Stress common ground of agreement (kindred feelings or desires);
(2) Stress that he is not there to force his views on the audience but rather to consider the problem with them;
(3) Indicate that he is approaching the subject with the point of view of his audience in mind;
(4) Mention that he is willing to share any sacrifice which might be involved;

(5) Explain how he at first opposed the project but later came to believe in it;

(6) Assert that he does not oppose an entire project or cherished principle but that he only proposes some modification of it;

(7) Say: 'If I was sitting among you, my thoughts would, I'm sure, be hostile. But up here, having the information I possess, my thoughts are very far from hostile. It will, therefore, be to your advantage to give me a fair hearing.'

19　Developing your voice

Where personality development is concerned, your voice is perhaps your greatest single asset. The voice has been recognised as such down through the ages. Here, for example, is some advice from a book written nearly three thousand years ago and found in a Pharaoh's tomb. The advice reads: 'Make thyself a craftsman in speech for thereby thou shalt gain the upper hand. The tongue of man is his weapon and speech is mightier than fighting.'

Demosthenes, one of the world's greatest orators, who lived in ancient Greece, went to great pains to develop his voice. He is particularly famous for delivering one of the greatest persuasive orations of all time, 'On The Crown'. His determination to succeed as a powerful speaker was so great that he would run up a mountain whilst rehearsing his speeches in order to improve his breath control. He would also practise speaking over the noise of the breaking waves on the seashore to improve the volume of his voice. And in doing this, he would speak with pebbles in his mouth to improve his articulation.

Demosthenes went even further. For whilst his voice was competing with the waves, he kept a dagger suspended over one of his shoulders so that the dagger would prick his shoulder every time he raised it. The dagger procedure was designed to make him breathe from deep down in his diaphragm, and not from the shallow level of his shoulders. This latter breathing is usually indicated by a raising of the shoulders.

Coming down the centuries to one of the world's greatest modern orators, Sir Winston Churchill, we learn that he also was determined to become a master of speech. Churchill's oratorical delivery was powerfully influenced by an American lawyer and politician of Irish descent, Bourke Cockran. In 1895, when Churchill was twenty-one, he stayed with Cockran for some time whilst he was on his way to Cuba to observe an insurrection which was taking place there at that time. Churchill many years later mentioned to Adlai Stevenson how Cockran had taught him how to use 'every note of the voice like an organ'.

Making Your Voice Powerful

Whilst you do not have to imitate the techniques of Demosthenes, why not set yourself a goal of further developing the wonderful instrument of your God-given voice. Become an artist in its use. Learn to tune, control, and play it to its best advantage.

I am not talking about changing your natural accent. For, provided your voice is clear and distinct, your accent will give character to your delivery. Indeed some too obviously trained voices can sound very artificial. People with such voices have over-identified with technique and have failed to acquire the 'art that conceals art'.

Apart from developing your voice to its full potential, you will need to do some work on it if it has any of the following disadvantages: too high-pitched; too soft-spoken; too harsh; inclined to slur (running the words into one another); inclined to mumble or to 'swallow' the ends of sentences; no control of breath (not enough breath and jerky breathing); no variety (a monotonous way of speaking); an exaggerated voice (usually too much prolongation of the vowels); omitting final letters in words (for example, the letters d, t, and k, and also the g in words ending in 'ing').

Voice Practice as Therapy

> *Let me speak and I will sweat this poison out of me.*
> — SPURGEON

The great American preacher, Spurgeon, on feeling unwell, would often say the above words. He realised that the use of the voice in certain ways can be a powerful tool in helping us to keep healthy. Speech exercises can act as a kind of therapy after a day's work which has been frustrating and tense. They can provide us with an outlet for the expression of our emotions, and help us to get our minds off our troubles. Apart from, of course, the added advantage of developing that powerful voice.

In doing the exercises which follow, a sense of humour and patience is required on your part in order to let the actor develop in you. If you practise the exercises every day, just as a musician practises his musical scales, you will be developing the on-going quality of your voice. Remember, it is regularity of practice that is important.

Enriching the Quality of Your Voice

The vowels are the great enrichers of the human voice. This fact is well exemplified in those magnificent Italian operas which utilise to the full the power of vowels. Well-formed vowels give purity of sound, richness, and carrying power to your voice. As regards carrying power, consider how the Mohammedan Muezzin, from the top of his minaret, summons the faithful to prayer by prolonging the vowel sounds as he cries out — 'ALLAH, OU AKBAR. LA ILLAHA ILLALLAH..' ('God is great . . .').

The main thing to remember in producing well-formed vowels is to get your voice forward (up and out). There should be no swallowing of your vowels. The secret is to open your mouth wide when saying the vowels in your practice sessions and to imagine you are projecting them well forward in your mouth. Also, round your lips well for the 'O' sounds.

Say aloud the following exercises. (1) EE; AH; OO; OH; AW. (2) KA - KO - KEE - KOO (Repeat several times). (3) 'Thou art thy father's child'. (Say this phrase slowly giving full value to each word. Then experiment with emphasising a different word each time.) (4) Sing the sound 'AH' as you go up and down the scale. (5) Sing in a low prolonged note the sound 'OO' and then 'OH' and 'AH'. To develop projection of tone, send these sounds to a far corner of the room. These vowel singing sounds are particularly beneficial exercises for anyone who wants to tone down a voice that is too nasal.

Making Your Voice Clear

As mentioned above, well-formed vowels give purity, richness, and carrying power to your voice. Consonants, however, go hand in hand with vowels, but their role is to chisel out, mould, and shape your words. They help to make your voice distinct, clear, and crisp. If you 'swallow' your consonants, or omit them, your sounds will run into one another and your voice will not be clear and distinct.

Put 'fire' and conviction into saying the following exercises. As you say them, make an effort to keep the words clear and distinct and don't run one into the other. Give particular attention to the final letter in each word. Make sure to keep your mouth well open and your teeth apart — otherwise your voice will sound smothered.

B: club boots; tub bounces; 'I babble into eddying bays, I babble on the pebbles.' P: damp plate; ship pond. P.B.: bump boots; top bottles. B.P.: scrub paint; superb print. D: one dozen dinner dances; the tired donkey had a vivid dream. T: the tall table that troubled them all the time; the great town in winning gave tit for tat. T.D.: sweet dame; constant danger. D.T.: loud trumpet; round train. N: nearer and nearer the nasty nettles came. M: the bomb did not menace the calm mood of the prime minister. K: black kennels; bleak caves.

Plenty of practice with consonants is essential, so let us continue with some more. Plenty of force is required in saying the following: the peas go, pop, pop, pop; the ball bounces, bob, bob, bob; humble, mumble, bumble bee; the tap goes, drip, drip, drip; the shoemaker's hammer goes, tap-tap, tap-tap, tap-tap-tap; clop-clop, clop-clop, go the shoes of the horse; pick a poppy; he was excited about the fight; dink-dunk; tick-tack, ticka-ticka-tack.

Finally, we will conclude this section by practising some more consonants of the alphabet. G: big guess; bag glides. K.G.: black gown; park glen. G.K.: beg kings; snug kitchens. NG.G.: a strong gust of wind (use plenty of emphasis); ding-dong (a few times). F: his chief fortune was floating away on the foam. V: a brave victory in his native valley. F.V.: brief victory; chief vested interest. V.F.: five fields; brave folks. S: she sells sea shells by the sea shore. Z: he was surprised by the zest of the zebras. S.Z.: glorious zeal; delicious zest. Z.S.: it is not wise to recognise senators who do not sit in the senate. S.H.: fresh shoals of herring fish. L: a library literally littered with literature. R: round and round the rugged rock the ragged rascal ran.

Resonance: The Loud Speakers of Your Voice

There are hollow chambers or spaces in the chest, mouth, nose, cheeks, and forehead in which the sound of the human voice echoes and becomes greater, richer, and more beautiful. This echo effect is called resonance. It enables you to get the sound out with the minimum of effort on your part, and it also saves your vocal cords from being strained. A powerful resonant voice is within the grasp of most people. The following exercises will help you develop resonance. However, be careful that you do not strain yourself whilst doing them.

The Exercises
(1) Humming is a great exercise for developing resonance. First of all, take in a deep breath and then practise a sustained humming in a normal sustained pitch on the letter 'M' (MMMMMM). As you hum the 'M', be conscious of and feel the strong tingling vibrations in your nose and the warm tingle inside your lips. Keep your lips together as you hum, but your teeth should be very slightly apart. Make sure you project the sound well forward in your mouth as you hum. It helps if you imagine the sound tingling your nose and lips and this can be achieved by rubbing your fingers along your nose to feel the vibration and gently touch your lips also to feel the vibration. As you practise the hum, strive for its quality rather than its volume. If you are practising at home in the privacy of your room, you can close your eyes and then concentrate on the sound of your hum and its quality. This exercise is best done standing up.

(2) As you practise exercise number one above in a normal pitch, this time, however, try gradually to increase and decrease the power whilst maintaining the same pitch. (3) Try to hum on higher and lower notes. (4) Hum up and down the ordinary scale with a deliberately slow and smooth hum. (5) Cup your hands as if scooping up water. Then in putting your hands to your face, put your mouth into them and say with great resonance — making, meaning, mining, money, muffling. (6) Practise exercise number one as you drive to and from work. (7) Hum bugle calls. (8) Feel resonance in the chest while saying: glope; goat; gulp; guilt. (9) Feel resonance in the nose while saying: nation; naught; nymph; nerve; noon; nip; nut; oy-ng (a few times holding the 'ng' for a couple of seconds each time). (10) Practise saying the wasp-like 'ZZZZZZZ'.

The Tongue Twister

Your tongue can be your voice's best friend. However, if it is lazy and unfit, it will lead to muffled and indistinct sounds. It deserves to be trained just as much as we exercise the other muscles of our body. Here are some exercises designed to help your tongue muscles become fitter, more flexible, and more active in producing that powerful voice.

With your voice well placed towards the front of your mouth, practise saying: 'I will put my spoon on the tip of my tongue'. Repeat several times and as rapidly as possible the following series of letters: 't-t-t-t-t-t'; 'd-d-d-d-d-d'; 'j-j-j-j-j-j'.

Practise saying tongue twisters. They will give your tongue great flexibility and control over words. Say them slowly at first, then speed up when you are more familiar with them.

'Theophilus thistler the thistle sifter in sifting a sieveful of unsifted thistles thrust three thousand thistles through the thick of his thumb. See that thou thrust not these thistles through the thick of thy thumb.'

Practise further exercising your tongue by moving it round the circle of your lips and by moving it from side to side.

Exercising the Lip Muscles

To develop flexibility of the lips, practise the following: (1) 'While the whimsical whistler, whistling and then whispering, wheedles the while whipped wheels of the whig and the whimpering whining whelp on the whirligig was overwhelmed by the wheelbarrow.' (2) Say the sounds 'woo-ee'. With the sound 'woo', round and push out the lips as far forward as possible. With the sound 'ee', stretch the corners of the lips as far back as possible as if suddenly asked to show a broad grin. Do this about twelve times. (3) Practise reading aloud in a strong whisper, at the same time exercising the lip muscles as fully as possible and throwing the voice upward and outward. (4) Say a prolonged 'Shhhhhh' a few times as if you are in a room where a baby is sleeping and someone has just come in. The practice of these exercises can be helped by moistening the lips beforehand.

Energising Your Voice

More breath control is needed for voice projection (as in singing, speaking in public and reading aloud) than is needed in ordinary conversation. It is, however, a common fault of untrained speakers to continue speaking until their breath is exhausted and then to gulp in air. This is usually accompanied by jerky and nervous speech and by a raising of the shoulders. The proper method of breathing for effective speaking is known as the 'Intercostal-Diaphragmatic Method'. It makes use of the full capacity of the lungs and the outgoing air is controlled by the action of the lower rib-cage muscles.

The great preacher Spurgeon once said: 'The next best thing to the Grace of God for a preacher is oxygen.' Proper breathing is not only the foundation for developing resonance in the voice, but it is also very beneficial for our health.

Here are some breath control exercises to practise. Be extremely careful, however, to avoid any strain while doing them.

(1) Keeping your shoulders down, put your hands on your lower ribs. Breathe in slowly and silently through the nose without feeling any strain. Let the rib-cage move upwards and outwards as you breathe in and let the diaphragm muscle expand until you can feel your stomach muscles pressing against your belt. Breathe out slowly through the nose letting the rib-cage go in slowly.

(2) After inhaling through the nose, practise counting aloud whilst exhaling. Don't strain for too many numbers.

(3) Breathe in slowly through the nose. Then breathe out whispering the sound 'Ah' — keep the sound steady throughout. While doing this try and feel the sensation of warming the vowel sound and feel composed as you breathe out. The late television personality Richard Dimbleby once said that the effective speaker should give warmth to the spoken word.

(4) Inhale slowly through the nose. Exhale quickly through the mouth.

(5) Inhale quickly through the nose. Exhale slowly and deeply through the mouth.

(6) Inhale through the nose until the lungs are nearly full. Pause for two seconds. Then take more air into the lungs — without straining. Exhale until the lungs feel empty.

(7) Practise blowing (as if blowing up a balloon) giving three short blows and then a long one.

(8) Inhale during four steps when walking, hold the breath for the next four steps, and then exhale during the third four steps.

(9) Take in a deep breath and then exhale softly on 'Ah'. As you exhale, stop the breath sharply every three seconds and hold it for three seconds before continuing on.

Developing the Actor in You: Using 'P-E-R-P'

Pause
Practise saying the following exercises out loud, and pause where indicated. (1) 'Poor, gentle, patient, noble Nell (pause) was dead.' (2) 'But suddenly (pause), as I approached the house (pause), he turned and ran away.' (3) 'Once upon a time (pause) of all the good days of the year (pause) upon Christmas Eve (pause) old Scrooge sat busy in his counting house.' (4) 'They also serve (pause) who only stand and wait.' (5) 'And thousands had sunk on the ground overpowered (pause), the weary (pause) to sleep, and the wounded (pause) to die.' (6) 'I am surprised (pause), amazed (pause), dumbfounded (pause) at what you're suggesting.'

Emphasis
Practise saying the following exercises out loud and emphasise those words which I have indicated for emphasis.
(1) 'They were both EXECUTED. Their fate was DREAD-FUL.' To emphasise the gruesome in this, slightly muffle the voice when saying the words 'executed' and 'dreadful'. (2) 'While STANDS the COLOSSEUM, ROME shall stand; when FALLS the Colosseum, Rome shall fall; and when ROME FALLS — THE WORLD.' Here the emphasis is building up to a climax which expresses the importance of Rome. Get great roundness into your saying of the word 'Rome'. (3) 'If you GIVE happiness, you shall also RECEIVE happiness.' The words 'give' and 'receive' are given special emphasis to show up the contrast.

(4) 'Scrooge thought and THOUGHT, and THOUGHT it over, and OVER and OVER, and could make NOTHING of it.' The words 'thought' and 'over' are each repeated three times in order to emphasise how much thought Scrooge was giving to the matter. Your voice must also reflect this hesitating thought of Scrooge when saying the quotation out loud. (5) 'Men, women, and children, ALL were put to the test.' (6) 'When I was a CHILD, I SPOKE as a child, I UNDERSTOOD as a child, I THOUGHT as a child.' In this quotation the word 'child' needs only to be emphasised at the beginning. To emphasise it more than once would be to over-emphasise. The emphasis is transferred in the rest of the quotation to the words related to the word 'child'.

Here is a very powerful exercise. Say it five times, emphasising a different key word each time. 'I did not say he stole the money.' The first time you say this sentence, emphasise the word 'I'. The second time, emphasise the word 'SAY'. Then, the words 'HE', 'STOLE', 'MONEY'. Note how the meaning changes each time you emphasise a different word in this same sentence.

Rate

Develop variety of rate by reading aloud from literature. When doing this, vary the rate as follows: Use (1) a slow pace for reverent or solemn pieces and (2) a quick pace for amusement, gaiety, excitement, impassioned appeals.

Pitch

Say the following sentence slowly on the lowest note possible: 'When I consider how my light is spent ere half my days, in this dark world and wide.' Take a good breath before saying it.

Say the following exercises on a high pitch, and rapidly. The first exercise expresses joy and happiness, whilst the second expresses a mood of violent hysterics. (1) ' "A merry Christmas, God save you", cried a merry voice.' (2) ' "Off with their heads", shrieked the queen.'

Say the following sentence out loud on a high pitch and keep your voice up until the final word 'it': 'Their voices rise up, their fists clench tight at the idea of victory, these people: they love it: and the more exciting it is, the more they enjoy it.'

Improving a Monotonous Voice

People whose voice tends to be monotonous should practise reading aloud from dramatic plays. Here, however, is a little exercise which should help us awaken those 'vocal emotions' in the voice. I call the piece 'Moody Jane'. Try and express the various emotions in it.

> One moment in the day, Jane would be really happy, bright as the sun. The next moment, however, utter hopelessness and dark despair would take possession of her soul. Then, as if by magic, her voice and eyes would sing and laugh, oh such a merry rippling laugh. Then suddenly, however, her mood would change yet once again and she could become angry or jealous. Sometimes her voice can be as sharp as steel. Finally, her mood becomes quite romantic, and she thinks of moonlight and roses, and her voice becomes soft and lovely.

Toning Down a Shrill Voice

People whose voice tends to be shrill or jerky should practise reading aloud from prose or poetry which expresses quietness, tranquility, or meditation. While doing this they should prolong the vowels a little longer than they would in ordinary conversation. It helps to imagine that the vowels are being 'warmed'. Try this piece of prose.

> One quiet Summer's afternoon, as Jane sat in her rose garden, she thought, 'How lovely it is to become part of nature, part of the air, the summer breeze, the gentle rays of the sun.' She could feel the grass growing, the gentle movement of the trees, and the sweet scent of the roses. Then softly and silently, she fell asleep.

Practise Reading Aloud

An effective way of developing your voice is to practise reading aloud as often as possible using the principles of 'PERP' already referred to in this chapter and in the chapter 'The Script Speech' (see page 95). Your reading aloud can embrace poetry, plays, and prose.

Poetry

The reading aloud of poetry is especially good for awakening your vocal emotions. Poetry has to be read aloud to do it justice — the poem on the page does not really come alive unless it is read aloud. Having selected a poem, read it carefully to grasp its meaning. Become aware of its sensory images. For example, having silently read Wordsworth's 'The Daffodil', close your eyes and visualise the cloud, the lake, the breeze, etc. Try and capture in your imagination the experience of the poet. Now speak the poem aloud and as you do so try and convey these sensory images. Taste the words just as you taste a good wine. Savour the experience.

Plays

When reading aloud from a play, experiment with your voice by changing it to indicate the different characters. As you do this, also give expression to the underlying feelings of the words. Get under the skin of the characters. Use gesture where appropriate.

Prose

With regard to prose, bear in mind that your vocal punctuation will sometimes differ from the written punctuation. So, having selected a piece of prose (from a book, newspaper, or magazine), read it aloud first to get a feel for its meaning and to decide where you will pause. Then practise reading your prose piece in a standing position as if addressing an audience. Hold the book about chest high at a reasonable distance from you. And as you read aloud, occasionally look up from the book in order to increase your eye-contact with that imaginary audience. You can achieve this by letting your eyes sweep ahead as you are reading to see what words are coming next, or by taking in a number of words during a pause and then saying them while looking up.

Also bear in mind that, apart from using PERP (pause, emphasis, rate and pitch) in your reading aloud, you should aim for clarity of expression — this means pronouncing the final letters in words and not slurring or running words into one another, for example, 'frinstance' instead of 'for instance'.

Finally, why not practise reading aloud from this book. Apart from helping to develop your voice, it will also help you to remember the various points in each chapter.

Part Four

MEDIA COMMUNICATION

Once a word has been allowed to escape,
it cannot be recalled.
— HORACE

20   Speaking to the Press

The gallery in which the reporters sit has become a fourth estate of the realm.

— THOMAS BABINGTON MACAULAY

Writing a Press Release or Report

The Press may have only enough space to publish the bare bones of your press release or report. They are generally not interested in exhaustive descriptions of events, or in long lists of names. The first paragraph, therefore, should be self-contained, brief, and include the essential facts of your story built around a basic theme, such as, an important decision reached at a meeting. It should, where relevant, answer Kipling's famous questions — What? Where? When? Who? How? Why?

WHAT?	What meeting? What event? What happened? To decide what? What was learned? What organisation? What decisions were reached?
WHERE?	Where did the event or meeting take place?
WHEN?	When did it take place?
WHO?	Who was involved? Who were the principal speakers?
HOW?	How did it happen? How was it organised? How were the decisions reached?
WHY?	Why do you think it happened? — this question tries to uncover the real cause of the problem or event.

The succeeding paragraphs in the release or report should consist of a more detailed account or development of the basic facts contained in the first paragraph.

Organising a Press Conference

First of all, ask yourself — is it really necessary? Call a press conference only when it is justified. Assuming that yours is justified, consider the following points.

Timing

Ask yourself: In what edition of the papers do I want this story to appear? Having answered this question, time your press conference accordingly. Don't rush the Press.

Invitations

Issue invitations to the news editors and appropriate correspondents of the papers, periodicals, TV, radio, and so on, who are likely to be interested in your event or story. In your invitation, explain briefly what the conference will be about. Where relevant, include an advance extract from the principal speech (or summary of it) with an embargo that it is not to be published until after the speech has been delivered.

Venue

Ensure that the room or auditorium is suitable enough to accommodate everybody, together with all the equipment, such as microphones, etc.

Briefing Your Appointed Spokesperson

Your spokesperson should know all the necessary facts and figures relating to the story or event and the organisation's line or policy on it. He or she should also have replies ready for anticipated questions, including the awkward ones. The answers to these should be written down and rehearsed. It is also well to remember that everything will be 'on the record' for the media (that is, it might be published or broadcast) unless the speaker gives an indication that the item is 'off the record' — 'I wish to make a statement off the record . . ..' There is, however, no guarantee that every single reporter will honour your request.

Have a Trial Run

Allocate responsibility to the various people for specific areas of the press conference, such as who will chair the conference, etc. Have a trial run when these areas of responsibility have been allocated.

The Press Kit

Issue a press kit to each representative of the media. The kit, where appropriate, might contain such basic information as: the background to the news-makers; the history, aims and objectives of the organisation; some photographs, biographical details of the organisation's leaders, and so on; brochures; annual reports; the full text of the principal speeches. If a press kit is not issued, it would be advisable to offer a press release in its place. This press release could be placed on each representative's chair, handed to each one as they arrive, or handed out at the end of the briefing.

Refreshments

Refreshments should be appropriate to the occasion. There is, however, no need to be lavish. The story is the vital point in any press conference.

Initial Briefing of Press

At the beginning of the conference, tell the Press how much time is available for questions.

Answering Questions

In answering questions, you should stick to the point of the question and avoid repetition or straying into areas about which you are uncertain. As you answer the questions, be careful that you don't belittle the questioner. Be courteous and try to answer the questions to the best of your ability, no matter how stressful and pressing they might be. As far as possible, avoid saying 'No comment', as the wrong implications might be read into this phrase. If relevant you could say, 'An investigation is currently under way and until the findings are known, I have no comment to make.' For further hints on answering questions refer to the chapters 'Radio and Television Speaking', and 'Understanding Logic — Putting on Your Logical Armour'.

The Follow-through

Give the media representatives the name, address, and telephone number (day and night calls) of a spokesperson who is capable of giving any further information that might be required.

21   Radio and television speaking

Whenever members of the general public are presented with an opportunity of speaking on radio or television, this is usually to take part in an interview, a panel discussion, or a phone-in programme. The following hints are designed to help you understand and prepare for the 'ordeal' a little more comfortably. First of all, realise that the reality is always less dreadful than the contemplation of it. Most people leave a TV or radio studio with a feeling that it was 'not so bad after all'. Also remember that if you are well-prepared and concentrate on getting your points across, you will probably forget to feel nervous. Preparation is important, whenever possible, because every 'um' and 'er' will make you sound indecisive.

The TV Studio

A television studio can be somewhat offputting. There is the searchlight glare of the studio lights and the accompanying heat they generate. In addition, there is the mass of equipment — cameras and microphones, and TV technicians all around you. There is usually a number of cameras in order to give a variety of shots. Make-up is usually applied by the make-up people because without it the intensive lights would make your skin look very pale and the heat would make your face shine a lot.

During rehearsal (if there is one), the studio people test and adjust the lighting in order to get the best picture possible. Any necessary adjustments to the set and the props are also made during rehearsal. The director tells the performer which moves, if any, to make and which camera to face. For example, a performer appearing on a specialised programme to demonstrate some skill will be given instructions about movement and how to face the camera.

'Line-up' time is the period which comes after rehearsal and which immediately precedes recording. Final advice is usually given by the producer/director during this period.

The Television Camera

If you are required to face the camera, such as in most 'straight' TV talks, remember to look at the lens — the camera in use is usually lit up. As you look at the camera, don't let your eye-communication become vacant, for then you will seem to be talking past or through your viewers, and you may appear as having 'shifty' eyes! The secret is to look at the lens of the camera as though they were the eyes of a person and to talk as naturally and sincerely to that person as you can, in a pleasant and lively way. This practice helps to give some animation to your TV presentation. Flexibility can be achieved by moving the head occasionally but, in doing so, still keep your eyes on the lens.

If you are being interviewed, there is no need to face the camera. Regard it as an eavesdropper. Look at the interviewer and avoid looking down or away from him.

Newsreaders give the appearance of nearly constant eye-contact because, apart from the notes in their hands, the scripted news is generally passing in front of the camera lens as the newsreader speaks.

The Studio Microphone

The TV microphone will usually be suspended on an arm over your head (boom microphone), or hung around your neck, or concealed on your person. With the radio microphone, the studio producer will probably tell you the correct distance to position yourself in relation to it.

The Radio or TV Phone-In

As you prepare your phone-in question, comment, or reply to a question, the main point to remember is that brevity on your part is essential, as time is usually an overriding factor where the producer is concerned. So prepare well by writing out your piece and then prune it to the minimum. Rehearse saying it aloud several times.

If you are asked a question for which you have no prepared answer, avoid 'ums' and 'ers'. Instead, pause for a moment after the question has been asked, briefly think out your reply, and then give your answer as frankly as you can.

Recorded Talks and Interviews

If your talk, comment, or interview is being recorded, it is possible that it might be edited by the producer prior to being broadcast. There is always the danger inherent in this that your remarks might be taken out of context.

The 'Instant' TV/Radio Interview

TV and radio move at a very fast rate. They thrive on the topical, on the urgent, on things of immediate importance. Consequently, if you are asked to speak on behalf of your organisation, the invitation might well be within hours of the programme 'going out'. In addition to the short notice, more likely than not you will be allowed a very brief time to make your point. Here are some hints to help you acquit yourself reasonably well on the occasion:

Be Natural

Be yourself and speak your mind as frankly as possible. Make sure that you use your normal conversational vocabulary, for there is the danger that the tension of the moment could make you appear pompous. Don't let the speed of the media disturb you. Any little nervousness you feel will help to keep you alert and on your toes. And remember the interviewer is not a god.

Prepare Well

If you have done your homework, it should help you to relax. As you prepare your comments on the topic of the interview, ask yourself: What do I hope to achieve? What one or two definite points do I want to make? — and make sure you get these across in the interview. Avoid being abstract. It helps if you mention a brief personal experience or a relevant example to illustrate your point.

Anticipate possible 'sticky' or provocative questions and prepare your answers to these. Where possible, ask the programme producer or researcher for the gist of the questions you will be asked or the areas of discussion to be covered, as this will help you in your preparation. Also ask (where relevant) the name of the interviewer, the duration of the interview, and whether it will be live or recorded.

During the Interview

When asked the questions, give the core of your contribution as briefly as possible. Never be tempted into a train of thought which you will not have time to pursue. Avoid repetition and the lengthy sketching in of a background.

Handling Questions

The interviewer's job is to get information. Indeed many radio and TV interviewers, especially those on current affairs programmes, will ask provocative questions in order to probe deeply into problems and to stimulate the listeners into thinking about these problems. The interviewer will try to get beneath the surface in order to find out what really happened or what someone really thinks. The interviewee, on such occasions, should be aware of the purpose of the interviewer and try to keep his or her head. In preparing for the interview, anticipate likely questions, including the controversial and provocative ones, so that you can plan your response. Looking at the list of possible questions might also indicate those areas where you need to bring along some back-up data.

During the interview, listen carefully to the questions you are being asked — there may be some underlying assumptions in these which you may want to challenge. . . 'Your question involves an assumption which is not true'. An interviewer may also try to extend or enlarge your point beyond its level of credibility and you will need to watch out for this, for example, the interviewer might say, 'Can we take it as a matter of policy. . .', or 'What you are saying is. . .'.

If you don't know the answer to a question, don't be defensive or make any attempt to bluff. Admit you don't know, without hesitation and without embarrassment. If you are asked a hostile question, try not to show annoyance or set out to discredit the questioner. Just stick to your point as forcefully as you can and correct any misconceptions on the interviewer's part.

Sometimes an interviewer might ask you several questions all at once, or put too many words into the question. You would certainly surprise him if you said — 'Would you please repeat the question?' Just simply answer as many of the points as you can remember.

If you don't want to answer a question, politely say so, for example, 'I don't wish to be unhelpful, but I can't pass comment on that as it is under investigation.' If the interviewer persists, you might reply, for example, 'You've asked me that question a number of times and I've already told you that I cannot pass comment.'

It may be possible to use some of the interviewer's questions to your advantage, for example, 'Your question brings me back to the point I want to make, namely that. . .' or, 'If by that you mean. . .', as you give your prepared answer.

If you are asked a very involved question that cannot be answered in a reasonable length of time, don't speak rapidly in order to cover every conceivable point. Instead, limit your answer to the bare essence of the question.

If the interviewer tries to put words into your mouth, you might say, for example, 'You say that, I don't say that.' Or, 'Naturally I must disagree with your question's line of argument. However, it gives me an opportunity of clarifying my position once again. . ..'

When you want to answer a controversial question with a 'yes — but' or 'no — but' reply, it can sometimes be more effective to give the qualification first before giving the 'yes' or 'no'. The reason for this is that if you give your 'yes' or 'no' reply first, the interviewer may not allow you the opportunity of giving your qualification.

Here are some other helpful phrases in answering difficult questions: (1) 'I find your question very important, but very difficult to answer. We have not, as yet, enough information or evidence on which to base a satisfactory conclusion. However. . ..' (2) 'On this question, I can only give a personal opinion. . ..' (3) 'Much as I dislike evasive answers, I can only say. . ..'

Always be truthful. A 'cover-up' is usually easily detected and one lie generally leads to another. Remember — 'What greater crime can an orator be charged with than that his opinions and his language are not the same.' *Demosthenes*. Acknowledging the truth on a point allows you more time to develop your overall argument.

Finally, the chapter entitled 'Understanding Logic — Putting on Your Logical Armour' will help sharpen your mind in relation to answering questions.

Reading from a Script

Having a full script will cancel out 'ems' and 'ers'. However, reading a script can sound artificial unless you try to make it sound as natural as possible. Always use your natural voice and speak as if you are talking to just one or two listeners or viewers in the relaxed intimacy of their livingroom or kitchen. Think of these listeners or viewers and try to forget about the surrounding studio equipment. This was the approach used by President Franklin D. Roosevelt (of the 'New Deal' policy) during the financial crises of the 1930s in the United States. When he broadcast his famous 'fireside chats' on the radio to his fellow Americans, he visualised a group of two or three people listening to him as they sat around the fire.

A talking style may be developed by knowing the material so well that you can frequently look away from your script towards the microphone or the camera lens. Some broadcasters rest a finger or a pencil on the script to ensure that they don't lose their place in it. On radio, use appropriate gestures and facial expressions to suit the words you are reading, as this will reflect in your voice and help to prevent that 'reader's tone'.

Another useful technique is that of pausing briefly as if to find the right word. This helps to create the illusion of spontaneity. But whilst striving for variety in your reading, don't emphasise words by hitting them too hard. Emphasise rather by the correct use of pause, by varying your rate of speaking, and by using pitch changes. Good breath control is also necessary because breathlessness will be easily picked up by the sensitive studio microphone.

Sometimes a studio rehearsal takes place before a talk is broadcast so that the producer can time the talk and have the voice-level measured on the control desk. The producer, through headphones, can convey instructions or advice as it is needed. As you read your script, move your pages quietly to one side as you finish with them.

With regard to the setting out and reading of a script, see also the chapter entitled 'The Script Speech'.

The Studio Chair, and Movement

Sit comfortably. However, don't slouch in the chair in too relaxed a fashion as this can give the impression of an assumed TV superiority. And sitting too far forward appears nervous. Lean forward, however, when you want to emphasise a point.

As regards movement and gesture, remember that *too* much of these can look artificial and overpowering to people watching in the intimacy of their livingroom.

The Studio Discussion

When invited to take part in a studio discussion, find out from the producer or researcher who else will be taking part, as this will help you when preparing your points. Bring along some brief notes or relevant data which will help you check out crucial facts or statistics during the discussion. Having notes with you, even if you keep them in your pocket, can give you a feeling of confidence.

Ignore the cameras and talk to the programme presenter or the other members of the discussion group. Only the presenter talks directly to the camera to address the viewers. During the discussion, if you disagree with the person speaking, you can attract the attention of the presenter by shaking your head in disagreement. This is a mild form of heckling. Avoid interrupting a speaker you oppose. Instead, cut in when he pauses for breath by saying, for example, 'There's a point I'd like to make. . ..'

The Interview in the Street

You may sometime be stopped by a radio or television reporter and asked your views on something or other, for example, a bus strike. The main thing to remember on such an occasion is that you have to make a definite and brief statement. There is usually no time allowed for lengthy preambles. You either agree or disagree with the bus strike. So state your view as succinctly as possible.

Part Five

DEVELOPING FLUENCY

One ought every day at least, to hear a little song, read a good poem, see a fine picture, and, if it were possible, to speak a few reasonable words.
— GOETHE

22 On becoming a fluent speaker

Seek not for words, seek only fact and thought and
crowding in will come the words unsought.
— HORACE

My dictionary defines fluency as a 'readiness in the use of words'. Fluent speakers have a ready supply of words at their command to express their thoughts. Many people, however, find it difficult on occasions to synchronise their words with their thoughts. They have some thoughts at the back of their mind, but often find it difficult to give expression to these thoughts in the right words. This is where fluency practice can help.

Where developing fluency is concerned, the words of Horace have a profound significance. They sum up a whole philosophy of communications training which suggests that if we get an idea from our mind, infuse it with our feelings, and then let ourselves go — the words will come. However, the more we practise fluency exercises, the more readily will the *right* words come. I now suggest various ways in which you can develop or further improve your verbal fluency.

Topics for Fluency Practice

Charles Dickens once said: 'The world is full of good subjects. All you have to do is to reach out and put a little salt on their tails.' Dickens is right. Not only is the world out there full of good subjects, but so also are you. Like everybody else, you are full of attitudes, beliefs, ideas, experiences, observations, facts. A good way of developing fluency is to draw upon your personal fountain of topics as if from a reservoir and to practise clothing them in your own words. Remember you will always be more fluent (whether in private practice sessions or in a class) when you speak on topics that interest you deeply. So, many of the topics I suggest below for fluency practice are aimed at stimulating your thinking on your various interests, and also to jog your memory. I am sure many of the topics will strike a chord with you.

155

The practice consists of picking a topic, jotting down or outlining a few ideas that strike you on that topic, and then speaking out loud on your outline of these ideas using whatever words come to mind.

How I keep fit

The day I. . .

A quotation developed

An appeal for. . .

My present job

A social problem

A film worth seeing

My first. . . (child, car, job, etc.)

An enjoyable holiday

A political party

My travel to work

A complaint

An ambition

How I conquered. . .

Why I am a. . .

A useful hint

My views on the future

A proud achievement

A current event

I'm a convert to. . .

A story about an object

This I have made. . .

If I were. . .

A proud possession

A deep conviction

My club

An absorbing book

A funny story

How I broke a habit

An observation

An unforgettable character

My hobby

A memorable event

For and against. . .

An embarrassing moment

My interest in. . .

My earliest recollection

I'm angry at. . .

My company's products

My locality

How to. . .

A utopian dream for. . .

Why I collect. . .

My pet

If you are describing an event or an experience, you might find it useful to cover all or some of the following: What happened? When? Where? How did it happen? Who was involved? Why do you think it happened? Is there a lesson or moral to be learned? If personally involved, how did you react? How did you feel about the event — then and now?

Here are some further topics for practice under the general

heading of 'favourites'. Pick some relevant topics, and in your practice talks say why they are your favourites. My favourite. . . poem; magazine; newspaper; prayer; menu; radio or TV programme; quotation; composer; writer; singer; charity; football team; politician; souvenir; book; sport; TV or radio personality; school subject; record; drink; poet; fable; music; actor/actress; sports star; pub; city; diet; motto.

Reading for Fluency

You can also turn your reading of books, magazines, and newspapers into a great opportunity for developing verbal fluency. After you have read a book, or an article from a magazine or newspaper, summarise it in a few sentences and give your own views. You might ask yourself, for example: What is the author's message? What are the implications of his message? How does the message relate to my own experience? Why do I agree or disagree with his message? Practise speaking your answers to these questions out loud.

Look at the 'Letters to the Editor' section of your newspaper. Pick a subject heading that appeals to you. Read the letter aloud and then speak your views on it — agreeing or disagreeing and giving your reasons. Do likewise for the editorial in the newspaper and for one or two of the major news items. As regards the news items, it can help your fluency if you imagine that a TV or radio interviewer has just said to you: 'Can you tell me briefly in the one minute remaining to us what are your views on. . .' (the news item you have selected from your newspaper).

Observe to be Fluent

Genius is a perception of the obvious which nobody else sees.
— ANON

Here are some observation exercises which you can use to some effect in furthering your verbal fluency.

(1) Look around a room and select an object at random. Observe it closely and write down all the ideas that occur to

you about that object — no matter how trivial. When you have listed a number of ideas, look at the first idea on your list and speak on it in the words that come to mind. When your flow of words ceases, go on to the second idea, and so on down the list.

(2) Make a tour of your house and examine the pictures on the walls. Describe the pictures and the meaning they have for you.

(3) Close your eyes and imagine you are bringing an audience on a tour of your house.

(4) List three things that happened to you today. Speak aloud about these.

(5) During the week, observe more closely the things around you — at home, on your way to work or college, etc. (traffic jams, noise levels, etc.). Practise speaking on these using the method suggested in (1) above.

23   The power of quotations
and seed thoughts

A beautiful thought beautifully expressed
is worth far more than any jewel.
— ANON

One of my interests, as you may have observed in reading this book, is collecting quotations, mottoes, and 'wisesayings'. I would recommend the practice to anyone interested in furthering their speaking career. A powerful, authoritative, and apt quotation in the right place in a talk can be very effective.

Most of the world's greatest orators have sprinkled their talks with appropriate quotations. Abraham Lincoln was one such orator. Probably no quotation has ever had more influence upon a people than the famous Biblical quotation he used in his Springfield, Illinois, campaign speech of 1858, when he said, 'A house divided against itself cannot stand'. Lincoln had spent several days searching for a suitable phrase which would present in the strongest possible way the proposition he intended to advance in his speech, namely, that his nation could not permanently endure a population half-slave and half-free — '. . .It will become all one thing or all the other.'

His political advisers recommended that he drop this proposition from his speech. It was, they said, 'very unwise', 'fifty years in advance of public opinion', and that it would kill Lincoln and the Republican Party. Lincoln's reply to his advisers shows the stature of the man, and his commitment to his convictions. He said: 'Friends, I have thought about this matter a great deal, have weighed the question from all corners, and am thoroughly convinced the time has come when it should be uttered; and if it must be that I must go down because of this speech, then let me go down linked to truth — die in the advocacy of what is right and just.'

Quotations in Your Talks

In looking for quotations for talks, you will find books of quotations in your bookshop or local library. Most of these will be indexed so that you can readily find quotes on most subjects. As you build up your stock of quotations, don't forget Biblical quotations. They are still very popular. This fact of the Bible's popularity was recognised by Cecil B. De Mille, famous for his great epic films based on the Bible. When he was asked why he made so many Biblical films, he is reported to have said, 'Why let two thousand years of publicity go to waste.'

How many quotations should you use in your talk? This will depend on your own discretion. The too frequent use of them, however, might lead your listeners to labelling you as a pedlar of other people's thoughts without an original thought of your own. They will want to know what *you* have to say. The main secret regarding their use, however, is that of relevancy. Don't drag in a quotation for the sake of the quotation itself.

The Magic of Seed Thoughts

Let us now consider how you might also use quotations to some advantage by developing them as 'seed thoughts'.

What is a seed thought? I am sure you are familiar with the saying, 'The child is father to the man'. This expresses a profound truth, namely, that great things are contained within small things in seed form. The acorn contains the future oak tree. Similarly a good quotation contains a universe of meaning in crisp capsule form waiting to be unlocked by the speaker in search of fluency of thought and expression. Quotations are teeming with seed thoughts crying out to be explored and developed.

We can develop these seed thoughts by working on them in a special way — as we shall see below. This work is important, for the practice of developing seed thoughts can help us to develop our own on-going liberal education and make us more fluent in the process.

You will gain far more from the exercise below if you especially develop those quotations that deeply appeal to you. Why is this? The reason is that such quotations strike some deep down chord within you. They, as it were, speak to your mental condition at particular moments in time. There are unexpressed ideas or seed thoughts within you that are akin to various unexpressed ideas in seed form in those quotations. So your collection of quotations can be used as a magnet in drawing out your unexpressed ideas on various topics, and in the process you will develop greater fluency of thought and expression.

How to Develop Seed Thoughts

First of all, look at your selected quotation and jot down in outline form the various thoughts it suggests to you. You might ask yourself questions about it. For example: What in general does this quotation mean? What do the individual words mean? Why has it significance for me? Does it have significance for others? What problem is the quotation expressing? What is the logical conclusion?

You might also use your imagination and try to visualise specific examples of the quotation's message and its possible application to your own life and to the world in general. Finally, practise speaking aloud on the written-down outline of those seed thoughts which you will have generated from the quotation. In doing this, speak aloud as if explaining your collection of thoughts to an audience.

You will, incidentally, find that each time you come back to practise on the same quotation, new thoughts will flow to the surface of your consciousness more rapidly. And you will develop greater fluency on that quotation. Ponder on this: 'A preacher never gets the real message out of a sermon until he has preached it half a dozen times.' *Knox Little*

Seed Thoughts for Practice

Why not try your hand at developing the following seed thoughts — if they appeal to you.

The truth shall make you free. *The Bible*

Happiness is the achieving of a goal of your own choosing. *Anon*

Man is a complicating animal. He only simplifies under pressure. *Robert Townsend*

Nothing in the world is more powerful than an idea whose time has come. *Anon*

All the animals except man know that the principal business of life is to enjoy it. *Samuel Butler*

Nothing should be prized more highly than the value of each day. *Goethe*

War is nothing more than a reflection or image of the soul. It is the fiend within coming out. *William Channing*

In every mark of genius we recognise our own rejected thoughts: they come back to us with a certain alienated majesty. *Emerson*

There is no such thing as inevitable war. If war comes it will be from failure of human wisdom. *Bonar Law*

Faith is one of the forces by which men live and the total absence of it means collapse. *William James*

Fanaticism consists in redoubling your efforts when you have forgotten your aim. *George Santayana*

To live is to change and to be perfect is to have changed often. *Cardinal Newman.*

Democracy is the worst form of government except all those other forms that have been tried from time to time. *Sir Winston Churchill*

Struggle is the law of growth; character is built in the storm and stress of the world. *Will Durant*

Where there is no vision the people perish. *The Bible*

Life is not a matter of having more, but of being more. *Pope John Paul II*

Powerful Action Quotes

In collecting and developing your quotations as seed thoughts, you will notice that the wording of many of them will be action orientated. Below I give some examples. Why not develop as seed thoughts any of these that appeal to you. The action content, however, will become more meaningful if you try to live the quote's message for a week. Think deeply about it, let the seed thoughts develop in your mind, and commit the quote to memory. Recall it at intervals during the day — and act on it. It could change your life.

Decide what you believe in. . . Find something you want to do, then if it's permissible, you've damn well
got to do it. *Sir Charles Snow*

No sooner said than done — so acts your man of worth. *Quintus*

Friends are like flowers, they need cultivating. *Angus Ogilvy*

Softer than the flower where kindness is concerned; stronger than the thunder where principles are at stake. *From the Vedas*

People who cannot find time for recreation, are obliged sooner or later to find time for illness. *John Wanamaker*

Relax, enjoy and, most of all,
love your children. *Dr. Benjamin Spock*

They can conquer who believe they can. *Virgil*

Earn affection by attention. *Anon*

I will lift up mine eyes unto the hills from whence
cometh my help. *Psalm 121*

This too shall pass away. (There are many stories and legends about the origin of these words. The legend I like the best is the one that says the words were thought out by the wisest men of an ancient kingdom in order to help the king meet every problem and situation with courage and wisdom.)

24 The impromptu talk – speaking on the spur of the moment

It usually takes me more than three weeks to prepare a good impromptu speech.
— MARK TWAIN

Do you have a natural ability to speak on any subject on the spur of the moment? Most people don't have that ability. From my own experience in the field of communications training, I know that the majority of people can only become effective speakers if they are willing to pay the price which is careful preparation of their talks. If someone seems to you to be giving a successful 'impromptu' talk, whether at a political, business, or community meeting, it is very likely that they have already given that subject some deep and serious thought, or they may have delivered a similar talk on a previous occasion. They mentally draw from this previous experience or from their already prepared remarks for this occasion. For example, one of Sir Winston Churchill's critics is supposed to have claimed that Churchill gave the best years of his life to thinking up his spontaneous remarks. Mark Twain, as my quote implies, was obviously of the same school. If I were to summarise the attitude of this school, it would be: the greater the orator, the more careful his or her preparation.

Impromptu speaking occasions, however, have that happy (or unpleasant) knack of catching up with us from time to time. So it is in our interest to have a little training in it. I believe anyone can become an effective impromptu speaker with a little practice and guidance. Let me show you how to achieve this ability.

Anticipate Being Asked to Speak

It is a wise practice to prepare and rehearse a few words for any occasion or function at which you think there is any possibility that you might be called upon to speak. Examine the agenda of a meeting and ask yourself questions, for example: What are my views on the various items? What problems are likely to arise at the meeting? Then write down, using a few headings in outline form, your answers, comments, views, on the various issues. Rehearse speaking on your outline and as you do so, aim for brevity and simplicity.

At meetings, get into the habit of making occasional notes of what the other speakers are saying, so that you may refer to, build upon, or criticise their remarks if called upon to speak. Write out notes on points of conflict or uncertainty at the meeting and then give your solutions to these. You might also decide to define the terms used in the meeting and give explanations.

Limited Time for Preparation

If you are at a function or speech competition and you are given a limited amount of time to prepare, try the following. First of all, consider carefully how you might start and how you might end. Then, make a quick decision and select one or two points which you can make on the topic and sandwich them in between your introduction and conclusion. Knowing how you are going to end means that you can lead straight into your conclusion when the competition warning bell rings, and this also gives a high degree of confidence.

Impromptu Speaking Training

Practice in impromptu speaking is extensively used in effective speaking classes as a means of training participants to think quickly and to improvise in communication situations. Class participants are expected to make some apt remarks on a topic given to them by their instructor. In speaking on such topics, there is usually a number of approaches open to speakers. You may:

(1) Relate the topic to some personal experience by saying, 'I remember. . .' and then tell a story which illustrates the message you want to develop.

(2) Relate the subject to something with which you are already familiar, such as your education, your reading, your job, your family, your hobbies, your ambitions, etc. For example, if you

are given the topic 'Architecture', you could comment on the fact that, as the end user, you live in a house designed by an architect. You could then go on to comment on the features you like and dislike about your house, for after all, as Aristotle said, 'The wearer of the shoe knows where it pinches.'

(3) Ask questions — what? when? where? how? who? why? — relative to the subject. The answers are then given.

(4) If relevant, mention the cause and effects of the topic problem and offer a solution.

(5) Briefly sketch in the past, present, and likely future of the topic.

(6) Give a few of the pros and cons of a topic problem and mention where your own preference lies.

(7) Divide the topic into categories (social, economic, political, etc.) and say you are going to speak briefly on one of those categories.

(8) Make an appeal for action relevant to the topic.

Impromptu Speaking and Mental Blanks

It is not uncommon to have a momentary loss of words or a mental blank when giving an impromptu talk. If this happens, try performing some simple action such as taking a sip of water, blowing your nose, or asking your audience a question related to what you have been saying. As you are doing this, your mind would be searching for the missing thought. This is stage managing yourself and rescuing the situation.

25 Listening and conversation

Nature has given to man one tongue but two
ears that we may hear from others twice as
much as we speak.
— EPICTETUS

Two men, each of them a little hard of hearing and unwilling
to admit it, were travelling on a train in England. The first man
said to the other, 'Is this Wembley?' The second man replied,
'No, it's Thursday.' Whereupon the first man said, 'So am I.
Let's have a drink.' This little story illustrates the point that very
often we assume we are being understood when in fact we are
not. For real understanding and good conversation to take place,
the ability to listen effectively plays a vital role.

There are two main reasons why we are often poor listeners.
First of all, we fail to make the effort to pay *real* attention to the
person speaking. Secondly, because our listening speed is much
faster than the speed at which people speak, we are tempted to let
our minds wander and consequently miss what the speaker is
saying. Then, when we realise that we have been wandering, we
mentally fill in what we consider to be the details we have missed
— and we are very often wrong in our assumptions regarding
those details.

What can we do to utilise this time difference between
listening and speaking? How can we keep wandering to a
minimum? Here are some ways which should help improve your
listening and conversational ability.

Listen Actively

As you listen to the person talking, mentally repeat back to
yourself the key ideas the person is expressing. This practice will
help you understand, consider, and remember what he or she is
saying and enable you to make appropriate responses. Listening
and understanding is also facilitated if you pick up the
underlying feelings behind the person's words. Indeed, the tone
of a person's voice can often be more revealing than the actual
words used.

167

You might also consider observing other non-verbals, such as: facial expressions; hand positions; body posture and movement; degree and duration of eye-contact and silences; and, finally, how the person likes to manage their own personal space. Observing the various non-verbals is important because the words the person uses very often have their own surface meaning, whereas the non-verbals can convey an entirely different message. And this non-verbal message is very often the true message. The person might say, for example, 'I'm not complaining' but his or her non-verbals might indicate otherwise. In this regard actions often do speak louder than words. Observing the underlying feelings and the other non-verbals of the speaker will enable you to make appropriate responses. With regard to your own non-verbals, your nodding and your eye-contact can give active encouragement to a speaker.

If you decide to make a verbal intervention, there is a number of options open to you. You can reflect back feelings, ask questions, or clarify points. Let us consider each of these in turn.

Reflect Back Feelings

You are reflecting back feelings to a person when you use phrases such as: 'You must have felt pretty good about that'; 'I understand'; 'I see'; 'You feel deeply about that, don't you?'; 'I can see how that would upset you'; 'Is that so?'. Reflecting back feelings indicates to the person that you understand him or her. It also helps the person to examine his or her feelings on the subject of conversation. In this regard, you have probably often observed how the experienced TV or radio interviewer allows people to ride with their feelings for as long as possible. They often achieve this by waiting out on pauses. Counsellors also, in listening to people with a lot of annoyance in their system, very often allow these people to let their feelings flow out before recommending any course of action.

Good listeners who reflect back feelings are developing the gift of empathy, that is, they are becoming 'in feeling' (from the Greek 'Em Pathos') with someone. Some people have this gift by nature. They intuitively or unconsciously understand the feelings of another person. We can often develop this gift of empathy by role playing another person in our mind. For example, a salesperson might use his or her imagination to visualise a customer or client and the various problems they have. Empathy can also be used to cheer up someone who is feeling down. In this instance, the person with empathy would first of all express sympathetic awareness of the person's problems and then behave cheerfully towards that person.

Ask Questions

There are two types of questions you might ask, namely, the open question and the closed question. A closed question would be, for example, 'Do you like your job?' This question is closed because it generally receives a 'yes' or 'no' answer. Open questions, on the other hand, generally allow far more scope for the person to open up, for example, 'How do you feel about your job?' or, 'What aspects of your job do you enjoy most?'

Other open questions might be: 'Then what did you do?'; 'How did you feel about that?'; 'Have you any ideas as to how you might handle it differently?'; 'Then what did you say?'; 'Could you elaborate on that?'.

Clarify Points

You can clarify your understanding of what was said by asking the person questions such as: 'Am I right in saying that you. . .?' or, 'As I understand it, the main point you're making is. . ..'

Converse Openly

We can also improve our conversational ability by engaging in personal disclosure and by giving feedback. Let us look at these factors in more detail.

Use Personal Disclosure

Personal disclosure means that you are willing to share some of your own deep thoughts and feelings with another person. This practice serves a very useful purpose. First of all, it helps you to get a deeper appreciation and understanding of your own thoughts and feelings. Secondly, this sharing tends to encourage a reciprocal move on the other person's part. Thirdly, personal disclosure generally helps to build up trust between people.

However, how open should you be about yourself? The degree of your openness will depend on your awareness of how helpful you feel such openness will be to both parties. In this regard, remember the advice of George Washington: 'It is an art to say the right thing at the right time, but far more difficult to leave unsaid the wrong thing at the tempting time.'

Give Feedback

You can help the conversation along by giving the person feedback on how his or her remarks are affecting you in the here-and-now. For example, 'I find that hard to believe' or 'I'm amazed at that' or 'That's wonderful'. Also listen out for 'throw-away' remarks and possibly ask the person to develop these.

It is possible that a person may have some previous 'unfinished business' on his or her mind which is preventing him or her from actively engaging in the here-and-now conversation. If this is so, saying to the person 'You seem miles away' can help the person to open up and dispose of the 'unfinished business'.

Finally, when you yourself are speaking, see if the other person is really listening to you. You might need to seek feedback by asking the occasional question, for example: 'Do you understand what I mean?' or 'Are you with me?'

26 Debating – the verbal duel

A debate is a formal system of argumentation designed to uncover as many as possible of the pros and cons of a particular question. Formal debates occur mainly in legislative assemblies, the council chambers of local authorities, and in debating societies where motions are proposed, debated (for and against), and finally a vote is taken.

Debating offers an exciting and challenging opportunity to exercise and sharpen your powers of reasoning. It forces you to clarify your mind on issues, and in trying to convince an audience, you develop a more vigorous personality in the process.

Here are some hints on debating procedures and techniques to help you become an effective debater and/or debate organiser. The chapter 'Understanding Logic — Putting on Your Logical Armour' is a complementary chapter to this one and it should also be read by the aspiring debater.

The Chairperson's Role

Most debating societies which meet regularly will have some administrative work to discharge ('Minutes' and perhaps some matters of 'Private Business') before the Chairperson introduces the public business of the debate proper.

After 'Private Business' has been concluded, the Chairperson reads out the rules of the society governing debate (if necessary) and places the Proposition or Question before the House. He might say, for example: 'The motion before the House tonight is. . .. It will be proposed by Mr Smith and opposed by Mrs Brown. Mr Jones will also support the motion and Mr Murphy will oppose. I now call upon Mr Smith to propose the motion.' Supporters and opposers are alternately called.

After both teams have been heard, the Chairperson usually throws the question open to the House. Any member of the House then wishing to speak for or against the motion may usually do so at the discretion of the Chair. This is usually for a limited period, the duration being indicated by the Chairperson.

When the time allocated for speakers from the floor is up, the Chairperson calls upon the leader of the opposing side to sum up. After this, he calls upon the leader of the proposing side to sum up. Proposers of motions usually have the last say or right of reply.

The Chairperson then calls for the decision of the judges or the vote of the audience on the motion in accordance with whatever procedure is being adopted. He then sums up the debate and, if he wishes, expresses his own personal views on the motion. He may then call for a vote of thanks to the teams. The leader of the winning team usually replies to this vote of thanks and in his reply praises the opposing team for putting up such a good performance. The leader of the other team says a few words of thanks in return.

Finally, the Chairperson thanks the audience for their attendance, the speakers for taking part, the judges (if any), and he then closes the meeting.

The Role of Judges (if present)

Judges assess debaters on the quality of their debating. They usually judge on the basis of —

> Logical Presentation (the selection and development of the issues and the supporting evidence — its quantity and quality).
> Speech Delivery (conviction, sincerity, enthusiasm, clarity and projection of voice).
> Teamwork (the co-ordination of a team's arguments with no unnecessary overlapping by team members).

Proposing the Motion

The proposer usually begins by defining the words of the motion, revealing the fundamental issues as he sees them, and by outlining the essential arguments concerning those issues. If there is a team of supporting speakers with him, he usually deals in some detail with just one of the fundamental issues and leaves the remaining issues to be covered by the other members of his team.

In his summing up at the end of the debate, he briefly rebuts the main arguments of the other side, and then goes on to reiterate the original main arguments of his own team. He should not, however, introduce any new matter into his summing up.

Opposing the Motion

The opposer of the motion usually begins by stating any points of agreement with the proposer and he then goes on to outline the issues he (and his team) have chosen. If there are differences in the selection of the issues, he shows how his selection is more fundamental than that selected by the proposer. The opposer then usually develops one of his selected issues, and leaves the other issues to be developed by members of his team.

In his summing up he would follow the same advice as that given above for the proposer's summing up.

Refutation

The best and most enjoyable debating is usually a nice blend of a well-prepared speech plus the cut and thrust of rebutting (or criticising) the arguments of your opponents. When your own arguments are rebutted by your opponent and you in turn explain and defend your own case, you are making what is called a 'rejoinder'. So when you refute your opponent, you have an opportunity to pull down (rebut) his arguments and to build up (rejoin) your own.

However, as you verbally duel with your opponent, remember that it is sometimes wise to concede a scoring point made by him as this practice will very often have the effect of weakening his point. Also bear in mind to take careful notes of his main points. In doing this, accurate recording is vital as this will avoid the risk later on of being accused of distorting his words. A useful hint in recording is to divide a sheet of paper vertically in half. On the left hand side write down his points and on the right hand side your possible replies to these.

Finally, it is usual for an experienced debater to rebut (with a few sentences at the opening of his speech) what the previous speaker on the opposing side has said. The inexperienced speaker, however, may decide to launch out immediately with his prepared speech and to leave rebuttal to the more experienced speakers on the team.

Secrets of Rebuttal

The usual method of engaging in rebuttal is as follows. First of all, state clearly to the audience what it is you propose to rebut. Then show where your opponent's argument is faulty and consequently not to be accepted. Its lack of credibility will usually be based on some or all of the following —

Not sufficient data produced to prove the point

The data is not relevant

The data is out-of-date

The source of the data is poor, unreliable, biased

The arguments produced do not support the conclusion (show up logical fallacies, etc.)

Finally, recall the attention of the audience to the real issues at stake and show how you have proved your interpretation of these issues.

The Debating Brief

Where a debating team is concerned, it will greatly enhance their teamwork and the overall logical presentation of their case if they prepare what is known as a debating brief. This is a logical outline of the whole case which a team prepares before each member of that team gets down to working out the intricate details of his or her own speech.

The debating brief ensures that everything each member says will fit into the context of the team's total presentation. The team comes together and, under the direction of the team leader, prepares the brief. When the brief is prepared, the team as a whole may help each individual member in developing that part of the brief assigned to them before they finally put it into speech form. A brief consists of the following:

The Exordium or Introduction

In writing out the introduction to the brief, the team first of all states clearly the motion to be debated. They then define the various terms in the motion (dictionary definition, common usage, specialist usage, historical usage). Sometimes the history of a question might be looked at (for example, capital punishment) in order to see what the terms mean in the light of that history.

Determining the Issues

The issues are the major points on which belief will depend. The team asks: What are the central and crucial issues of the debate? In determining the fundamental issues, the team should avoid concentrating on any points of minute details which are not likely to be seriously challenged. The team also asks: What will the other side admit or not admit? What are the possible strong arguments on the other side?

The Proof of the Issues

Having listed the fundamental issues as they see them, the team then brainstorm the evidence for their interpretation of these issues. Wherever possible, the evidence produced should be within the experience of the audience.

The Peroration or Conclusion

This consists in restating the arguments and the proof in summarised form. For example: 'Therefore, since we have shown you that. . . (mention the first issue) because. . . (summarise the evidence in support of the team's interpretation of that issue) and secondly, that. . . (mention the second issue) because. . . (summarise the evidence in support), you must support (or oppose) the motion that. . . (mention the motion or proposition).'

Diplomacy in Rebuttal

Debaters should confine themselves to attacking their opponents' case rather than attacking them personally. Win a debate if you can, but don't humiliate. And if you lose the debate, be a good loser and accept the outcome. As someone said, 'To lose graciously, is to achieve a victory.'

Anticipating the Opposition

The team should consider possible points which their opponents might make. These points, with answers to them, should be written down on cards which may then be referred to during the debate if the opposing side do in fact make these points.

Another useful practice during preparation is to write down on one side of a piece of paper the arguments for the motion and on the other side the arguments against. The pros and cons can then be examined for their strengths and weaknesses. Or, sometimes a team might decide in their presentation to mention some of the arguments against their case in the hope of drawing some of their opponents' 'sting'.

Speaking from the Floor

Do not be put off by the fact that previous speakers from the floor may have covered the points you had in mind to say. Go ahead and make your contribution in your own words and warmly endorse any points you agree with. In the minds of the audience your contribution will be seen as another voice strengthening those points you support.

Part Six

SOCIAL AND
SPEAKING OCCASIONS

*Strangers are just friends you don't
know yet.*
— HELEN KELLER

27   Toasts and after-dinner speaking

The company makes the feast.
— ANON

The term 'to toast' means to drink to the health of someone or some thing. How the word 'toast' first came to be applied to this pleasant and ancient custom is interesting. Apparently, during the reign of Charles II (1660-1685) it was generally believed that a piece of spiced toast in the glass of wine gave the wine a better flavour.

Toasting and speech-making at formal dinners or banquets have always been productive of goodwill and friendship. The speeches that grace such occasions are frequently very powerful instruments in binding an audience together whether at local, national or international level. Golden opportunities are presented for re-kindling the latent enthusiasm towards the common interest that brings the group of diners together.

The diners themselves expect to hear speeches — in fact they would feel cheated if there were not any. Unfortunately, however, many social occasions are spoiled by long boring speeches which seem to 'get in the way' of the entertainment which generally follows. The speeches, like the wine and the cigars, should sparkle and stimulate. In order to help your speech do just that, I give below some hints which should help you enjoy your meal that little bit more, knowing that you have properly prepared your brief after-dinner 'vocal cocktail'.

Effective After-Dinner Speaking

First of all, it should help your confidence to realise that an after-dinner audience is usually the most relaxed and sympathetic of all audiences. They are usually in a very receptive mood, having been mellowed by the good food and drink, the sense of occasion, and the friendly companionship of their fellow-diners. You capitalise on this by including some light-hearted remarks or stories in your speech, especially at the

179

beginning. (Regarding humour, see the chapter 'Humour in Speech'.) The speech itself should be brief, easy to understand, and generally pleasant, although it may contain a serious message.

Allow your audience the opportunity and the time to react to what you are saying. You achieve this by speaking fairly slowly and by making frequent use of the pause. Do, however, vary the pace from time to time as your subject matter might dictate. Your actual pausing will be influenced by a 'feel' for your audience's reaction, by interruptions of applause, quips thrown at you, laughter, the occasional 'hear. . .hear', and possibly some 'restrained' bangings on the table. Pause momentarily when these happen. Enjoy them with your audience and take full advantage of the opportunity they present for bringing the audience along with you.

As you rehearse your speech before the actual occasion, bear these possible pleasant interruptions in mind, and allow for them when timing your speech. And as you prepare your material, avoid incorporating anything that might possibly embarrass anyone who will be present on the occasion. The main part of your speech will generally be related in some way to the objectives of the dinner or to the objectives of the organisation sponsoring the dinner. It should also be spiced here and there with the occasional humorous story or anecdote relevant to the occasion. When you deliver your anecdotes, don't rush them. Instead, relax and enjoy them with your audience; savour them. Your audience are relaxed and they will be only too willing to laugh with you. However, when you wish to introduce a serious note, you could use a transitional phrase such as: 'And now, Mr Chairman, may I dwell, just briefly, on a serious matter. . . (pause as you let your audience adjust to the different tone). . . I refer to. . ..'

In concluding this section, I would like to make a brief comment on luncheon talks, as distinct from after-dinner occasions. Luncheon talks generally deal with specialist business issues and toasting is not generally a part of the proceedings. Some humour, however, has a very useful part to play in these talks and can help to make them more entertaining. With regard to timing, both speakers and organisers should remember to keep the talks within the time limits as most members of the audience will have some afternoon appointments to keep.

The Toastmaster

The organisers of very formal dinners sometimes engage the services of a professional Toastmaster who will announce the various toasts. However, as most 'ordinary' dinners don't have the eloquent services of a Toastmaster, the Chairperson of the evening will announce the speakers. In this regard, a speech of introduction is not usually required from the Chairperson in announcing the proposers and responders.

The Toastmaster (if present) usually stands behind the Chairperson, makes the necessary announcements, and calls upon the various speakers. In doing this, he 'knocks' (that is, strikes a mallet on the table — usually three times) to call the diners to order, and, in ringing tones, makes his announcement, for example: 'Mr President (or Mr Chairman). . . (then the various dignitaries), Ladies and Gentlemen, please see that your glasses are charged and pray silence for Mr . . . who will propose the toast of. . ..'

Grace before the meal will, of course, be said by any clergyman present.

Forms of Address

Local embassies, religious houses, government departments or VIP's secretaries, will usually supply any necessary data on dignitaries and also the correct format for addressing them when commencing a speech.

Proposing a Toast

Begin your proposal by saying, for example, 'Mr Chairman. . . (the dignitaries), Ladies and Gentlemen . . . It is a great pleasure for me to propose the toast of. . .' (the subject of the toast). Then say in your speech why it is a pleasure. The usual length of this speech is about five minutes. When you are concluding your speech, take your glass and say: 'In conclusion, Ladies and Gentlemen, I ask you to join with me in drinking to the health of. . .' (name of the person toasted). Or, if you are toasting an organisation or a theme, conclude by saying, 'In conclusion, Ladies and Gentlemen, I give you the toast of. . . (name the organisation or theme), and I couple with this toast the name of. . .' (Name of the person who is going to reply. Be sure to give the name in full with the various distinctions attached to it). The diners then rise and repeat the toast after you. Whoever is being toasted will, however, remain seated. The Chairperson or Toastmaster then calls upon the responder. As a general rule there should not be long gaps between each toast.

Replying to a Toast

Although you will have your speech of reply prepared in advance, it is usual on the actual occasion to refer briefly to some of the remarks of the proposer before you deliver your prepared speech.

Begin your reply by saying, for example, 'Ladies and Gentlemen, I'm happy to reply to the generous welcome you have given this toast.' Then thank the proposer for his or her kind wishes and express your pleasure at being invited to speak. Having covered your main points, conclude by offering your best wishes to the organisation or people concerned.

The Loyal Toast

This is the first toast and is proposed after the coffee has been served. The Chairperson ensures with the waiters that all the glasses are filled. He or she then rises (possibly having been announced by the Toastmaster) and simply says 'The President', or, 'The King', or, 'The Queen', as the case may be. The diners having risen, repeat the words after him or her, drink the toast, and then sit down. As there is no reply to this toast, the Chairperson immediately gives permission to smoke, and allows a minute or two for 'lighting up' and for settling down before the next toast is called. Note that smoking is never allowed before this toast.

28   Wedding speeches

The bride and groom, assisted by their parents, welcome the arriving guests at the place where the reception is being held. After dinner is announced, Grace is said by the clergyman who officiated at the ceremony. Prior to the speeches, telegrams (if any) are read by the best man after the coffee has been served. He then calls on the various speakers in turn.

There are usually three toasts — to the bride and groom, to the bridesmaids, and to the parents of the bride and groom. However, it might be desirable to propose other toasts, for example, to 'Absent Friends'.

Toast to the Bride and Groom

The toast to the bride and groom is proposed by the bride's father or by a relative or old friend of the bride. In this toast, the bride's father might cover some of the following points: (1) 'Rev. Fr., Ladies and Gentlemen, it is a great pleasure for me to propose this toast to. . .' (first names of bride and groom). (2) Refer to the happiness of the occasion. (3) Welcome your new son-in-law into your family; mention how well suited the couple are to each other; their achievements; anything of interest they have planned for the future; possibly how they met each other (if novel); personal reminiscences of the bride and groom. (4) Thank the guests for coming. (5) Conclude by saying, for example, 'I'd like you all to join with. . . (name of bride's mother) and I in wishing. . . (first names of bride and groom) prosperity, long life and happiness always. Rev. Fr., Ladies and Gentlemen, I give you the toast of: The Bride and Groom.'

Response by Bridegroom, and Toast to Bridesmaids

The bridegroom replies on behalf of his wife and himself. You might cover some of the following points: (1) 'Rev. Fr., Ladies and Gentlemen, on behalf of. . . (wife's name) and myself, I'd like to thank. . . (name of father-in-law) for his very kind wishes.' You could then comment on some of his remarks. (2)

Refer to the occasion and its meaning for you. (3) Thank the bride's parents for their kindness to you and for the reception they have arranged. (4) Express your gratitude to your own father and mother. (5) Thank the best man for his help. (6) Thank the guests for their good wishes, for coming to the reception, and for their presents. (7) Thank the bridesmaids for the charm they have brought to the occasion and for their assistance to your wife in her preparations. (8) Thank the priest or minister of religion. (9) Conclude by proposing a toast to the bridesmaids as follows: 'It is my pleasure to propose a toast to the bridesmaids that they may have a long, healthy, and prosperous life. Rev. Fr., Ladies and Gentlemen, please rise and drink with me to the health of our bridesmaids.'

Response by Best Man, and Toast to the Parents

The best man replies to the toast to the bridesmaids. In your reply you might mention some of the following points: (1) 'Rev. Fr., Ladies and Gentlemen, on behalf of. . . (first names of bridesmaids), I'd like to thank. . . (first name of bridegroom) for proposing the toast to the bridesmaids. I fully endorse everything he has said about them.' (2) Talk about your friendship with the bridegroom going back over the years (when you first met, at school together, and so on). (3) Conclude by saying, for example, 'I'd like you all to join with me in wishing long life, health, and happiness to Mr and Mrs . . . and Mr and Mrs . . . (parents of both bride and groom). Ladies and Gentlemen, to the parents of the bride and groom.'

After this toast, the best man calls upon the clergyman who officiated at the wedding to 'say a few words'.

Best Man's Announcements

After the speeches, the best man makes any necessary announcements concerning the arrangements for the entertainment. He announces an interval and mentions the time at which the entertainment or dancing (opened by the bride and groom) will commence. He also mentions the name of the person who is to act as master of ceremonies for the entertainment, that is, if he is not performing this function himself. He then announces that the guests are free to leave the dinner table.

29   Speaking engagements

Proposing a Vote of Thanks

The effective way to prepare and deliver a vote of thanks (a proposing or a seconding) is as follows. Listen carefully to the talk, and as you do so, select and jot down one or two points that interest you. Build your vote of thanks around these points. For example, 'Mr Chairman, Ladies and Gentlemen, Mr . . . made two points in his talk which particularly appealed to me. First of all . . . Secondly, . . . In conclusion, Mr . . ., I enjoyed your talk very much, and so I'm delighted to propose (or second) this vote of thanks.'

As a general rule any disagreement with the speaker should be kept out of votes of thanks. To mention a disagreement would frustrate the purpose of the talk which is 'to thank the speaker'. Be brief and sincere. The proposer should sit in a strategic position such as at the end of the first row (near the wall) either to the left or to the right of the hall. When the proposer stands up to speak, she can then turn her back to the side wall and be in a position to have eye-contact with the platform and with the entire audience.

Judging a Competition

You might cover the following: (1) Speak of the value of such competitions and the qualities needed for success. (2) Say how much you enjoyed judging the competition. (3) Point out the merits of the best work. (4) Name the winners and make the presentation of the awards.

Opening Events

You might cover the following: (1) Express your pleasure in having been asked to open the event. (2) State your approval of the organisation responsible for organising the event. (3) Describe briefly the organisation's work and what it does for the community or for people generally. (4) Talk about the occasion and the place. Tell why the organisation needs funds. Mention the target, if one has been set. (5) Mention the various stalls, and be careful not to miss any from your list. However, if there are too many, just mention the different general categories of stalls. (6) Mention the entertainment and catering arrangements. (7) Speak about the co-operation and team-work that has brought all sections of the community together. (8) Finally, wish the event every success and then declare it open.

Accepting an Office

You might cover the following: (1) Say 'Thank you' and then talk about the work the organisation has done in the past. (2) Explain the principles or ideals of the organisation as you see them. (3) Say that you accept the office with a sense of responsibility. (4) Say that you intend to see its principles carried out to the best of your ability. (5) Express your intention of making contact with as many of the organisation's members as possible.

Making a Presentation

Here are some points you might make: (1) Speak about the reason for the occasion (to make an award to Mr White for . . .). (2) Elaborate on his achievement(s). (3) Describe the gift, its meaning, uses, history, etc. where appropriate. (4) Make the formal presentation. For example, 'On behalf of . . . (your fellow participants, the organisation, the committee, the company, etc.), I have great pleasure in presenting you with this token of our esteem (admiration, etc.).' Then hand over the presentation, shake the recipient's hand, and say, 'Congratulations'. Step back and listen to the recipient's words of acceptance. Never walk away immediately. N.B. Be absolutely sincere in your speech — never exaggerate.

Accepting a Presentation

Here are some points you might make: (1) Express your gratitude to the group (company, committee, etc.) for the presentation and for the kind wishes that accompany it. (2) Explain what motivated you in your work (service, deed, etc.). (3) Mention by name any others who have helped you and then thank them specifically. (4) Speak of the significance of the award and of how much it means to you. (5) Speak of the encouragement you feel as a result of this presentation and how it affects your enthusiasm and intentions for the future. (6) Possibly display the award and speak of its attractiveness and usefulness, etc. You might mention what you intend doing with it, for example, where in your home or office you are going to place it. (7) Finally, once more express your thanks for the award . . . 'I shall always cherish this gift and what it stands for. Thank you all very much.'

Retirement Presentation

You might cover some of the following points: (1) Say that it is both a happy and a sad occasion. Happy because everyone is here to congratulate . . . on his retirement, and sad because 'we're sorry to lose you'. (2) Mention his length of service with the company or organisation and some of the changes which have taken place during that time. (3) Brief biography of person. (4) Highlight some of his outstanding achievements or contributions to the company — things that made him 'special'. (5) Mention his intentions for his retirement and emphasise how busy he will be in his new life. (Avoid the 'well-earned rest' theme.) (6) Congratulate him and make the presentation.

Retirement Speech Reply

You might consider the following: (1) Express your thanks to the group for the presentation. (2) Say how much you have enjoyed working with your colleagues. (3) Thank the presenter for praising your accomplishments and thank those who have helped you over the years. (4) 'In conclusion, thank you all once again.'

Talk to Recruit Supporters

You might consider the following: (1) Tell your listeners that they will be joining a group of committed, enthusiastic, friendly people all of whom are dedicated to working together on a specific project. (2) Praise their qualifications for the job. (3) Mention the worthwhile experience they will be gaining.

Receiving a Presentation from a Club

You might consider the following: (1) Express your appreciation for the presentation. (2) Tell how much pleasure the club has given you over the years — the opportunities it presented to make good friends and to enjoy many happy occasions. (3) Say how delighted you are to have contributed to the club in any tangible way you could. Thank those who have helped you. (4) Say how much you will treasure their gift as a memory of this pleasant occasion. (5) 'In conclusion, thank you all very much.'

Talk to Fund Raisers

You might consider the following: (1) Introduce the literature that will be used on the drive and show the fund raisers how to use it and what points to cover during their canvassing. Possibly ask some of the fund raisers to role play what they will say. (2) List the main questions they are likely to encounter and suggest how to answer these. (3) Allocate the areas where they will operate and possibly give directions on how to get there. (4) Stress how important each fund raiser is to the success of the campaign. (5) Give the names and addresses of those people or co-ordinators who should be contacted in the case of any difficulties that might arise. In general, try and obtain definite commitments or pledges from the fund raisers. For further hints on this type of talk, refer to the chapter 'You as a Persuader — Techniques of Persuasion'.

Chairing a Lecture Meeting

The procedure is usually as follows. The speaker may be escorted to the platform by the Chairperson who would indicate by gesture to the speaker where he or she is to sit. When the audience has settled down, the Chairperson rises and introduces the speaker (see 'Introducing a Speaker' below). After the talk, the Chairperson thanks the speaker and then usually calls for questions. If questions are slow in coming, the Chairperson may ask an initial question in order to 'break the ice'. Sometimes the Chairperson (or it may be the speaker, by arrangement) repeats the questions asked by audience members. This practice very often clarifies a badly put or inaudible question, gives the speaker time to think out the answer, and enables those at the back of the room to hear the question. It is not necessary for the lecturer to stand while answering questions, provided, of course, that he or she can be seen by members of the audience.

Those questions should never be allowed which are offensive or abusive or which become excuses on which to 'hang' a speech. The Chairperson should stop attempts at speech-making if they are made.

The Chairperson may also limit the number of questions to one per person if he or she thinks it necessary to do so. When the time allotted for questions has nearly expired, the Chairperson may warn the audience that only one or two more questions can be allowed. After question time, the Chairperson thanks the audience for their questions and the speaker for answering them. There may then be a formal vote of thanks by a member of the audience, or the Chairperson may ask the audience to show their appreciation 'in the usual way'. (The Chairperson should always lead the applause — he or she sets the example.) If there has been a formal vote of thanks, the Chairperson thanks the proposer (and seconder if so), says a few words, and conveys the vote of thanks by saying, 'In conclusion, I'm delighted to convey our very sincere thanks to. . ..'

During the applause the speaker may give an indication to the Chairperson that he wishes to thank the audience, or the Chairperson may ask him if he wishes to reply to the vote of thanks. The meeting is then closed.

Introducing a Speaker

Here are some points which might be included in such a talk: (1) Welcome the speaker and announce the title of his talk. (2) Mention the speaker's qualifications and experience on his chosen subject. (3) Mention his particular relevance to the meeting, to the particular interests of his audience, and to this particular time or occasion. (4) Mention any connection he might have with the town or organisation. (5) Briefly mention his other interests (if relevant). (6) 'Ladies and Gentlemen, Mr . . .' (and lead the applause).

Be careful in your introduction that you don't commit the

speaker to any particular line of approach. Also, at this stage avoid giving your own 'pet' views on the subject. The usual length for a talk of introduction is about one minute. Finally, check with the speaker beforehand if he or she will take questions at the end of the talk.

Reading a Lesson in Church

Here are some general hints: (1) Rehearse the Lesson aloud several times beforehand. This will enable you to pinpoint any stumbling blocks and difficult pronunciations, such as place names, people's names, Biblical tribes, and so on. The Priest or Minister might need to be consulted with regard to these. Once you have decided on a definite pronunciation, stick to it. (2) Grasp fully the meaning of the words of the Lesson and let them have their impact on your feelings. (3) Know your cue when to come up to the lectern. (4) Stand confidently, and, before you read, check the microphone — a general rule is to have it 'just below the smile'. (5) Project your voice well forward, neither too loud nor too soft, and speak with conviction. (6) Don't rush the reading and remember the effective use of the pause. (7) Maintain eye-contact with the congregation as much as possible. (8) Finally, as regards your voice and the use of 'PERP' (pause, emphasis, rate, pitch), see the chapters 'The Script Speech' and 'Developing Your Voice'.

Speaking at a Job Interview

Preparation for a job interview will be enhanced if you rehearse speaking aloud your answers to the following questions (where relevant): (1) Why would you like to work for us? (2) Tell me about yourself? (Stress what you feel is relevant to the job). (3) What are your strongest qualifications for the job? (4) What were your reasons for leaving . . . (a previous job)? (5) What factors influenced your choice of . . . as a career? (6) What are your career objectives in the short term and in the longer term? (7) What do you consider has been your proudest career achievement to date? (8) What is your basic philosophy in relation to . . . (the type of work you do)? (9) If you were faced with a problem such as . . . (a problem related to the kind of work on offer), how would you go about solving it? (10) What future would you like to see for the industry for the next five years? (11) Any serious illness? (12) Tell me about your hobbies or interests. (13) What salary are you seeking? (Decide the minimum amount you will accept). (14) What notice are you required to give in your present employment?

It is also helpful to break your present job down into its major areas and to practise speaking on how you regard each of those areas. Finally, remember to relax and smile during the interview, use eye-contact, speak with conviction, express your interest in the job, and avoid being unduly negative about previous jobs.

Part Seven

MEETINGS AND COMMITTEES

*The first thing to do is to
form the committees.*
— T.S. ELIOT

Difficulties of a Statesman

30 The role of the Chairperson, Secretary and Treasurer

*Be sure to leave other men
their turns to speak.*
— BACON

A good Chairperson realises that most public meetings will contain some degree of conflict, as people will have their own opinions, one way or the other, on most issues. Free expression of these opinions is of the essence of democracy and is based on a natural fact, best summed up in the old Latin saying — 'Quot homines, tot sententiae' ('As many men, so many opinions'). Recognising this fact, the Chairperson should calmly and effectively conduct the meeting and not set out to dominate it. Here are some broad guidelines on the conduct of meetings.

Sequence at Meetings

Meetings generally include all or some of the following items, in order of sequence. (1) The 'Call to Order' by the Chairperson. In some organisations, an invocation or opening prayer, or indeed a roll call of members, is customary. (2) Miscellaneous Announcements (such as welcoming new members; passing on greetings; reading out apologies for absence; mentioning any alterations or additions to the agenda). (3) Minutes of Previous Meeting. (4) Matters Arising from the Minutes. (5) Correspondence Received (if any). (6) Reports (if any) from Officers or Committees. (7) Matters especially postponed to this Meeting and time from a previous Meeting. (8) Main Business or Motions (including any 'Unfinished Business' from the previous Meeting). (9) Date of Next Meeting. (10) Any Other Business. (11) Miscellaneous Announcements. (12) Programme Event (if any), for example, a lecture. (13) Adjournment.

Checking the Quorum

The term *quorum* refers to the minimum number of voting members required to constitute a valid meeting. It is usually fixed at a certain percentage of the total membership — about thirty per cent for a general meeting of members, or about fifty per cent for a committee meeting. The purpose of having a quorum is to prevent a small handful of people from dictating policy for the whole organisation. It also prevents a well-organised minority from rushing through unpopular measures at a meeting where they happen to have a temporary majority. A meeting should be adjourned to a future date if the quorum is not present within a specified time (10-15 minutes usually) after the time fixed for the meeting to begin.

Minutes

Minutes are the official records of the meetings of a committee or organisation. They enable members to know what was decided at previous meetings and they help to ensure that action takes place.

The Chairperson would say: 'Are there any corrections to the Minutes as read (or circulated)?' Only questions concerning the completeness or accuracy of the Minutes may be raised. If there are no corrections proposed, the Chairperson would say, 'Right, we can take the Minutes as read (or circulated) to have been approved.' Or, on more formal occasions, he or she might say, 'Will someone formally propose and someone second that the Minutes be adopted and signed.' The Secretary would then write in 'Approved as read (or circulated)', sign them and have them countersigned and dated in ink by the Chairperson. If the Minutes are to be corrected, the Secretary writes the amendment in the margin and asks the Chairperson to initial the correction, as well as signing the Minutes where it says 'Approved as corrected'.

Matters Arising from the Minutes

This item on an agenda ensures that motions passed by the members are being implemented and are not just left in the Minutes Book. The Chairperson, however, should not allow lengthy discussion on matters that have already been resolved. The Chairperson introduces the item by saying: 'Are there any questions concerning matters mentioned in the Minutes?' A member might say: 'Mr Chairman, has . . . been performed, and if so, what has been the outcome?'

Recognising Speakers from the Floor

Speakers must be 'recognised' by the Chair (obtain permission) before they may speak from the floor. The general rule is that only one speaker can be properly heard at a time. If several people wish to speak at once, the Chairperson should jot down their names and indicate the order in which he or she intends calling upon them to speak. In general, those who have not yet had a chance to speak should be recognised in preference to those who have. Once a speaker has the floor, he or she has the right to speak without interruption, unless some question arises relating to privilege (such as, the need to protect someone's good name), or to an emergency (such as, a matter of safety or personal comfort). The person interrupting would rise and say, for example, 'Mr Chairman, on a Point of Privilege. . ..' The Chairperson usually decides the issue.

Dealing with Motions

Most of the main business of a group or committee centres around the discussion of main questions or motions. There can be only one main question on the floor at any one time. The rules of an organisation may demand that motions be submitted in advance so many days before a meeting. All motions then received (if in accordance with the rules) would be placed on the agenda. If a meeting, however, cannot cover all the motions on an agenda due to shortage of time, these items would be carried forward to the next meeting.

In general, for most groups, the wording of a motion should be brief, simple, and phrased in the affirmative form, for example, 'Mr Chairman, I move (propose) that we have a club outing to . . . on the 25th of May.' Most motions also require a seconder. This ensures that at least one other person is interested in the motion, before discussion takes place. In general, speakers are allowed to speak only once on a motion. The proposer, however, usually has a right of reply before the vote is taken. He or she would reply to any criticism of the motion and answer questions raised by other speakers.

A main motion is usually considered as a whole, unless a motion is passed to consider it by parts. This might arise when a complicated motion is before the meeting. At informal meetings, motions often develop after previous lengthy discussion, when the Chairperson might ask members to put their suggestions in the form of a formal motion.

A member may ask leave to withdraw a motion which he proposed. This sometimes happens when a person senses, during the discussion, that his motion is not very popular and he does not wish to risk possible embarrassment by having it put to a vote. The Chairperson would immediately ask the meeting, 'Are there any objections to the motion being withdrawn?' If there are some objections, the Chairperson would ask for someone to move and someone to second that the person be granted permission to withdraw his motion.

Amendments

The purpose of an amendment is to 'perfect' a motion by either omitting, substituting, or adding something to it (words, sentences, or paragraphs) before it comes to a vote. Once a motion to amend has been proposed, seconded, debated, and successfully passed, the original motion as then amended is considered. If the amendment is rejected, the original motion is up for further consideration.

If an amendment to an amendment is proposed, seconded, and carried after discussion, the original amendment is altered accordingly. It is then open to discussion before being voted upon. If it is passed (and if there are no further amendments to the original motion), the original motion as now amended is voted upon. If the amendment to the amendment is lost, discussion will continue on the original amendment (and other amendments may be made on it) before it is put to a vote.

An amendment to an amendment cannot itself be amended. The reason for limiting amendments to one further amendment is to avoid excessive complication.

Points of Order/Information/Explanation

A member may interrupt a speaker on a 'Point of Order' when: (1) There has been a breach of the rules or standing orders of the organisation; (2) Any serious problem of procedure arises (for example, no quorum present; too much talking or whispering going on; a speaker exceeding the time allowed); (3) A speaker engages in: insulting language or swear words; personal abuse; irrelevancy (wandering from the issue); tedious repetition.

The Chairperson would ask the person raising the Point of Order to: 'Please state your Point of Order.' The Chairperson might then say, 'Your point is well taken' or 'Your point is not well taken.' If the Chairperson agrees with the Point of Order, he or she may, for example: (a) Ask the offending speaker to withdraw his or her remarks; (b) Ask the speaker to discontinue his or her irrelevant speaking and get to the point.

A member may also interrupt a speaker on a 'Point of Information', for example, 'Mr Chairman, on a Point of Information' or 'I should like to ask the speaker a question.' The Chairperson would ask the speaker if he objects, and if he does not, the Chairperson would say, 'State your question' to the person looking for information.

A member may also rise on a 'Point of Explanation' when he feels that he has been misunderstood or misjudged by another speaker, for example, 'On a Point of Explanation, Mr Chairman, I did not say . . ., I said. . ..'

Closing the Debate

A debate on a motion, or an amendment, may be closed in a number of ways. The Chairperson, for example, when he or she feels that a motion has been debated long enough, might say to the meeting, 'Do you wish the question to be now put?' If the reply is in favour, the Chairperson would then call for a vote on the pending question. The mover of the pending motion, however, is usually given a right of reply before the vote is taken.

Apart from the Chairperson, a member may call for a closure by saying, 'I move that the question be now put' or 'I move that we close debate.' If this motion is seconded, the Chairperson would put it to the vote.

If there is a lot of discussion and time is running short, the Chairperson might find it necessary to shorten the debate by: (1) Arranging a time-limit on future speeches; (2) Limiting the number of speeches from each side; (3) Announcing that the debate will close at a set time (a 'Guillotine').

At any time during a debate, a motion may be proposed to adjourn either the whole meeting, or a particular item or items of business, to a future date, time, and place. This might happen if tempers are hot, or if there is not enough information available for a decision to be taken on a motion.

Maintaining Impartiality — Order — Relevancy

The Chairperson at a public meeting should remain impartial and preserve order without bias. He or she should also ensure that everything said is addressed through the Chair. If a breach of order occurs, the Chairperson would say, 'The Chair calls the speaker to order.' Keeping order also involves disallowing members from engaging in cross conversations and from dominating a meeting (for example, 'Thank you for your views, but I suggest we let others have their say.').

If general disorder were to occur at a meeting, the Chairperson would use the gavel and call the meeting to order. If disorder were to continue, a warning might be given by the Chairperson stating that, if order is not restored at once, the meeting will be adjourned or suspended (for whatever period of time the Chairperson considers necessary).

Relevancy involves keeping speakers to the agenda, to the point, and to the time-limit. The Chairperson should inform members of the precise issues before them for consideration and what is in order at a particular time. A Chairperson might bring a wanderer back by saying, for example: (1) 'Mr . . . we are discussing . . ., not . . .. Please keep your comments to the point.' (2) 'I'm sure that's an interesting point, but you seem to be getting away from the subject. Please conclude.' (3) 'Time is moving on. Please get to the point.'

Closing the Meeting

The Chairperson usually summarises the meeting with regard to the decisions taken — who is to do what, when, where, and how and also what follow-up reports and meetings are planned.

The meeting itself is closed in any of the following ways: (1) 'The meeting is adjourned until . . .' (giving the date, time, and place of the next meeting). (2) 'The meeting is adjourned *sine die*' (no date set). (3) 'That concludes the business of the meeting. Thank you for your attendance.'

The Role of the Secretary

The Secretary is responsible for maintaining all the records of an organisation. This includes a list of members of the organisation, a calendar of events, the Minutes Book, details of the progress of sub-committees, if any, and all correspondence and publications. In addition, the Secretary keeps a petty cash book and cash box for small payments such as stamps, stationery, etc.

The Secretary confers with the Chairperson in the drawing up of an agenda for the meeting. The agenda, and any other necessary documents are usually posted to members at least ten days in advance of a meeting. It is usual to have spare copies of the agenda available at the meeting in case these are needed. The Secretary also brings to the meeting any other necessary documents, such as a copy of the constitution and rules, standing orders, list of members, etc. The Minutes and any other papers, documents, or correspondence that require to be read out at the meeting, will be read by the Secretary, who may also suggest what action, if any, needs to be taken on matters raised in the correspondence. Important letters dealing with items already on the agenda are usually dealt with under their appropriate headings on the agenda.

The Minutes of a meeting are written up under section headings (inserted in the left hand margin) which broadly correspond with the headings on the agenda to which they refer. The Minutes will also identify the meeting (name of organisation, committee, date, time, place of meeting, members present, apologies for absence). Also included will be the actual wording of any motions and amendments proposed, the names of the proposers and seconders, a brief account of the discussion, and the result of the voting for and against. The Minutes conclude by stating the time of adjournment. Copies of Minutes despatched to members of a committee often contain an action column on the right hand side which identifies by name the person who is to take action on particular items listed in the Minutes.

If at all possible, correspondence should be answered within twenty-four hours of being received. If, however, the matter requires the attention of the committee, the Secretary should acknowledge receipt of the correspondence and state that the matter will be dealt with as soon as possible. If the matter is extremely urgent, the Secretary, with the Chairperson's consent, would call a special meeting of the committee.

The Secretary drafts the annual report (usually compiled from the Minutes Book). It lists the main activities or highlights of the year, membership figures, brief summary of reports from sub-committees, and an expression of thanks to all those who helped in any way. The Secretary ensures that, where appropriate, each member receives a copy of the annual report.

Where lecture meetings are concerned, the Secretary engages the speaker, arranges the fee, notifies the speaker in writing of the date, time, and venue of the meeting, and gives any other information which might be helpful to the speaker. Such information might include: desired length of talk; names and topics of other speakers and their 'slot' on the programme; expected numbers; how formal is the occasion; any relevant phone numbers to contact, for example, the venue, in case the speaker is delayed; details of accommodation, if required; some literature on the organisation. As regards the venue, the booking of this should be confirmed in writing. The venue should also be checked for size, heating, lighting, ventilation, lectern, drinking water, etc.

The Role of the Treasurer

The Treasurer is mainly responsible for offering financial advice to the committee, for keeping and monitoring the accounts of the organisation, and for presenting the financial report at the Annual General Meeting. The Treasurer explains the organisation's financial position in relation to planned activities. He or she would have the objective of seeing that there is enough money to carry out the various activities and plans of the organisation. The responsibility for spending money, however, rests with the committee, and, ultimately, with the general membership. The Treasurer would also be the Chairperson (or at least an ex-officio member) of any financial sub-committee.

With regard to the accounts, the Treasurer: (1) Establishes an account in a bank named by the committee. This is usually a bank other than the one used personally by the Treasurer. A bank may want to see a copy of the Minutes which authorises the opening of the account. (2) Receives and records all monies paid to the organisation. (3) Collects members' subscriptions. (4) Submits all bills to the committee for their approval. The Treasurer pays these bills when they have been approved. The paying cheque will bear his/her signature and be countersigned by the Chairperson or by Trustees named by the organisation.

At ordinary meetings of the committee, the Treasurer reports on the amount of any income received since the last meeting, the amount of monies paid out, and the balance remaining. If there are new bills for payment he or she then brings these to the attention of the meeting. The Chairperson would ask for a member to propose the adoption of the accounts and the passing of the bills for payment. After these have been seconded and any discussion has taken place, the Chairperson would call for a formal vote.

The Treasurer presents the financial report at the Annual General Meeting. This embraces the annual audit — statement of income and expenditure, and the balance sheet. The accounts are usually audited by an independent auditor (perhaps a professional accountant) or by an auditing committee from the organisation.

Auditors will want to see that authority was granted for all payments made, that all figures are accurate, that receipts were issued and received for all transactions, and that all transactions were properly recorded in the books. They will also check to see that the balance in the books agrees with the balance in the bank and the cash box. In order to help them carry out their role, the auditors will usually scrutinise: (1) The various accounts books which record monies received and monies paid; (2) Petty cash books; (3) Receipted bills; (4) Stubs of receipt books; (5) Cheque books. Finally, if all is in order, the auditor or auditing sub-committee issues a signed and dated certificate stating 'audited and found correct'.

Conclusion

Language most shows a man:
Speak that I may see thee.
— BEN JONSON

In bringing this book to a close, let us reflect on its major theme, namely, how our speaking in everyday life can become more powerful and have more impact if we communicate with clarity, confidence, and conviction. This theme, the goal of all great speakers, has a long tradition and was perhaps most formally promulgated by the ancient Greeks. In their approach to education, the Greeks saw the supreme manifestation of their ideal of developing the 'Whole Person' as culminating in the perfect orator. Their dedication to philosophical enquiry, the arts, and the skills of oratory led them to lay the foundation stone of Western Civilisation.

In this book, I have placed emphasis on 'the mind behind the voice', for I believe the inner should powerfully guide the outer. Self-formulated convictions are vital in developing the all-round powerful speaker, for the difference between really great speakers and mediocre ones lies in the degree and force of their conviction about what they are expressing. As Emerson said, 'The eloquent person is one who is drunk with a certain belief.' In addition, the more we probe, analyse, inoculate and express our self-formulated convictions, the more we gain deeper insights into them. Politicians often discover this phenomenon at election time. The more the fledgling issues are effectively discussed with the electorate as the campaign proceeds, the deeper are the insights gained by both politicians and electorate into the evolving issues. In this triad of speaker/message/audience, the issues become clearer for all concerned.

We grow as human beings when we face problems from the vantage point of our convictions. They help us to face the reality of the 'moment of truth' with more equanimity of mind and with more possibilities for personal growth. It is precisely at these existential moments of decision, when we must express ourselves one way or the other, that further growth becomes possible.

Formulating our convictions forces us to make a personal enquiry into some of these 'moments of truth'. And in formulating and expressing our convictions, we avoid becoming a victim of mass thinking, or what George Orwell in his novel *Nineteen Eighty-Four* calls 'Newspeak' — 'Big Brother' has less of a hold on us.

Convictions, therefore, are the foundation stone of individual and personalised communication — the hallmark of the successful communicator. But built on this foundation must also be the ability to express the 'self' in a clear and confident way. Clarity of message can be achieved by identifying the *General Purpose* and the *Specific Purpose* of any communication. Concentrating on the GP and the SP prevents us from becoming involved and lost in incidentals at the expense of the essential message. These two friends of the communication process become the 'open sesame' to clarity of expression. Indeed, their application to life in general can lead us to some interesting discoveries — a 'eureka' experience. This is especially so if we bring a sense of urgency to our search for the general purpose and the specific purpose of things. This was the attitude, for example, of that charismatic communicator, Pope John XXIII. His simple message was to open the window and let a breath of fresh air into the Roman Catholic Church. The Second Vatican Council became that window. The concept of the general purpose and the specific purpose of communication will, therefore, help us to keep our sights on the essentials and prevent us from falling into that trap identified by the Roman dramatist Seneca — 'When a man does not know to what port he is steering, no wind is favourable to him.'

Regarding confidence, we saw earlier in the book how Disraeli made a disastrous maiden speech in the House of Commons. His speech on that occasion was longwinded and ornate, and his delivery lacked confidence. However, after being jeered by his fellow parliamentarians, he vowed that he would thenceforth speak in such a way that his colleagues would listen to his every word. He was helped in this objective by a veteran Irish parliamentarian, Richard Lalor Sheil (1791-1851). Disraeli's friend helped him to become aware of the secret of successful speakers, namely, careful preparation, brevity, and an ability to simplify the complex issue. Here is the advice Sheil offered Disraeli —

> Speak often, but shortly. Astonish them by speaking on subjects of detail. Quote figures, facts, dates, calculations. And in a short time the House will sigh for the wit and eloquence which they all know are in you. They will encourage you to pour them forth, and then you will have the ear of the House. . . .

This, of course, Disraeli did. Much of this advice, I feel, can still apply to modern parliamentary speaking which is frequently criticised for being too long, boring, and not sufficiently prepared. In this regard, parliamentarians, and indeed all of us who speak in public from time to time, can also learn a lot from another great speaker, Abraham Lincoln, and his passion for preparation, brevity, and simplicity. In addition, identifying our general purpose and specific purpose, as mentioned above, will also focus our speech research in the right direction. All of these factors breed that self-confidence which is the antidote for nervousness in speech.

I hope these pages have created in you a deeper awareness of the power of speech and how you may further develop your own power for good in this direction — whether it be for the good of your country, your community, your political party, your church, your work or business and, most importantly, for your own personal development. I should like to take this opportunity of wishing you every success in your speaking career.